Amy,
Thank :
in me!

WHAT GOOD IS
JESUS?

"Years ago there was a season when Christians ran around saying 'Jesus is the answer!' The problem was they weren't really listening to the questions. In his book, *What Good is Jesus?*, Marv Nelson listens to the questions and then lovingly shows how Jesus really IS the answer. Thank you Marv. This book will point many toward The Answer!"

- Dr. Ron Walborn,

Dean of Alliance Theological Seminary

"A fresh voice with a humble heart takes us on a journey of discovery. Marv asks us to reconsider Jesus and what He may mean to us in this day and this culture. I loved Marv's personal stories and his ability to help us see the potential connection of Jesus' story to our own story."

- Len Kageler, Ph.D.,

Author of *Youth Ministry in a Multifaith Society*

"Marv has been effectively working with and serving the millennial generation for years. And as a millennial himself, he has great insight into this generation. His goal in life is to live so authentically and vulnerably that his life truly demonstrates how God works in and through people."

- Kent Julian

Founder of Liveitforward.com

"In his second book, Marv Nelson writes from his passion both to see Jesus be real to people and believers real with one another. Marv candidly shares his own journey out of legalism to his desire to see the Church be real and authentic while working to bring positive change to humanity. Marv is not afraid to tackle subjects most authors and preachers avoid —religion, homosexuality in the church, and diversity, just to name a few. You will want to take your time going through this work, for it is not meant to entertain but to challenge you to not do church, or go to church, but to be the church!"

- Dr. John Stanko,

Author of *A Daily Dose of Proverbs*

"In *What Good is Jesus?*, Marv Nelson creates a necessary conversation that we need to be having with millennials in our churches. With bold transparency, Marv explores the beauty of who Jesus is while addressing cultural challenges for young and old alike. I'm thankful for this book personally and believe it will have a significant impact on our churches in the U.S."

- Tim Meier

Director of Sites for Envision

"Marv is passionate, humble, honest, and in love with Jesus. His heart overflows in these pages, and the result is a vital read for this generation and those seeking to reach it. Timely, accessible, and wise, *What Good Is Jesus?* is a powerful resource for the Church in these turbulent times."

- Jason Weimer

Co-author of *The Finishers*,
Cru Campus Field Staff in Pittsburgh, PA

WHAT GOOD IS JESUS?

MARV NELSON

Ambassador International
GREENVILLE, SOUTH CAROLINA & BELFAST, NORTHERN IRELAND

www.ambassador-international.com

What Good Is Jesus?

ISBN: 978-1-62020-552-5
eISBN: 978-1-62020-474-0

Cover Design & Typesetting by Hannah Nichols
Ebook Conversion by Anna Riebe Raats
Author Photograph by XTOphotography

AMBASSADOR INTERNATIONAL
411 University Ridge, Suite B14
Greenville, SC 29601
www.ambassador-international.com

AMBASSADOR BOOKS
The Mount
2 Woodstock Link
Belfast, BT6 8DD, Northern Ireland, UK
www.ambassadormedia.co.uk

The colophon is a trademark of Ambassador

To my children: Marvin Elijah, Amelia Naomi, and Liam James. May you experience the goodness of Jesus throughout your lives in tangible ways!

ACKNOWLEDGEMENTS

This book is in your hands, not because of one person, but because of several amazing people. First I want to thank my wife Hilary for all of her patience, kind words of encouragement, and help in the big vision for the book. I also want to thank Warren Bird for helping me make this book better, as well as his many years of encouraging me in this project. Another large group of people need to be thanked: those who gave to the Kickstarter to help fund this book coming to life. Your faith in me and your generosity is mind-blowing!

Finally, I'd like to thank Tim Lowry, Kendra Winchester, and the rest of the team at Ambassador. Tim, your faith in this book is what's letting it go to print and allowing it to come to life. Kendra, for your tireless editing of this project as well as very helpful insight on how to make it better! To all of you, I am forever grateful.

CONTENTS

FOREWORD

This very readable book will unlock several mysteries for you.

Marv Nelson wants to take you inside the mind and heart of 18-35 year olds, known as the millennial generation. Marv himself is a millennial and he leads a ministry that reaches millennials, but he also knows how to explain his generation to anyone wanting help to understand and engage them. He's on staff in a 140-plus year old multigenerational church and he speaks widely to others leading student and millennial ministries. Plus for many years, he's coached me in understanding his generation, which is why I was honored to write this Foreword.

The first mystery Marv unlocks is the question found on the cover of this book: "What good is Jesus?" Marv responds with sound theology and a helpful apologetic perspective, all framed through an enjoyable narrative.

Another mystery Marv helps readers with is how to frame relevant questions—and why that's important for millennials. He captures well the skepticism, honest inquiry, and distinct value base of his generation. He models well how leaders, by asking questions, can find greater responsiveness and receptivity. He follows the teaching model of Jesus who often created teaching moments by phrasing an insightful question.

Marv also unpacks how to be authentic and vulnerable, while keeping the focus on Jesus, not the speaker. Millennials often want to know if they can trust the messenger before they're willing to listen to the message. Marv demonstrates how he does that through his communication style.

A final mystery Marv decodes is the power of relationships in answering tough questions. The strength of having personal connections can help you, as Marv demonstrates, not back down from going after the tough issues millennials bring up.

Everyone has met—and likely been soured by—people more eager to talk than to learn, and more absorbed in their own knowledge than in discovering how their resources apply to someone else's context.

Marv embodies just the opposite. He's teachable and growing. He truly lives out his own words voiced in the opening chapter, "You and I, by our answers and by our reactions to questions that people pose to us, have the power of turning those in our generation towards God, or away from Him."

May God use the time you invest in reading this book – or in handing it to others – to make more and better disciples of Jesus Christ.

—Warren Bird, Ph.D.
Seminary Professor, Author/Coauthor of 28 books,
Research Director at Leadership Network

INTRODUCTION: HONEST QUESTIONS THAT CHANGE LIVES

I REMEMBER SITTING AT STARBUCKS when I received a phone call from Jacob[1], one of my leadership team students. He called in a semi-panic and asked if I was free to meet to discuss some questions he had about the Christian faith. I told him that I had time later that afternoon and he seemed relieved. As I hung up the phone I wondered, *What happened to him that caused him to be so shaken up about his faith?* I definitely considered him to be one of our strongest students in the faith. In order for it to shake him up, I figured what Jacob wanted to talk about must be pretty big.

Later that afternoon, he arrived and sat down and pulled out a notebook. He was taking a course at the University of Pittsburgh titled *Origins of Christianity* and the professor was not a Christian. This professor had brought up several debates about Christianity. Jacob told me that he had rarely, if ever, encountered these debates and began to drill me with questions as to how Jesus could be good and the only choice for faith if this litany of questions seemingly remained unanswered.

I began to answer his questions one by one, and in the midst of answering, I started thinking about how important these questions and their answers are. Jacob's case is not rare. Many people in our generation have similar questions, whether we are Christian or not. Some of us are taken away from the faith because they cannot answer these questions, or because these questions were answered for them incorrectly. Either way, many in our generation are seeking answers to deep questions when it comes to the goodness of Jesus and the validity

---

1   Not student's real name

of His claims. Doubt is a normal thing to happen in our lives, and we need people to help walk us through this doubt as well as find helpful answers to the deep questions that bring about our doubt.

After that day in Starbucks, I began to seek out other millennials to find out what common questions individuals in our generation are asking. During my investigation, I preached a sermon series based off of these questions to help those in our generation walk through this doubt and started writing a book to do the same. I desired to create a resource many of us could turn to in our doubts about the goodness of Jesus. In this book, I seek to relationally answer those deep questions as if you and I are at Starbucks sitting across from one another as I was with Jacob.

You and I, by our answers and by our reactions to questions that people pose to us, have the power of turning those in our generation towards God, or away from Him. After a while in ministry, when it came to my preaching and teaching, I realized that for a long time I just kept teaching the people in my care what *I thought* they needed to hear—not what *they thought* or what they actually needed to hear. I was not giving my fellow sojourners the opportunity to ask the questions burdening their hearts, so in turn I wasn't answering any of the real questions they had. In that moment with Jacob, I was struck deeply by this reality.

After reflecting on my apparent lack of teaching my fellow sojourners what they needed to be taught, or guiding them down the path they needed led, I realized that much of my ministry to them and with them had become an airplane safety check while riding in a car. The information is not bad, in fact it's helpful while in an airplane, yet that information is woefully irrelevant in a car! My teaching was completely irrelevant to millennials' current situations. I learned the hard way that I needed to bring some light to their "now" situations of doubt and struggle by answering their current questions. Maybe, if I had been teaching what they actually needed, Jacob wouldn't have been in such a panic when those questions came about in his class.

When Steve Jobs, known today as the founder of Apple, was thirteen years old, he had a conversation with his pastor that affected the rest of his life. Sadly, that conversation led to a decision that turned him away from Jesus. In the highly acclaimed book *Steve Jobs* by Walter Isaacson, we see this thirteen-year-old Steve ask his pastor a question.

> In July 1968, *Life* magazine published a shocking cover showing a pair of starving children in Biafra. Jobs took it to Sunday school and confronted the church's pastor, "If I raise my finger, will God know which one I'm going to raise before I do it?"
>
> The Pastor answers, "Yes, God knows everything."
>
> Jobs then pulled out the *Life* cover and asked, "Well, does God know about this and what's going to happen to those children?"
>
> "Steve, I know you don't understand, but yes, God knows about that."[2]

According to Isaacson, after this exchange, Jobs left church and never darkened another door. George MacDonald in an article titled *The Soul of Steve Jobs* about this interaction says: "For the pastor, that brief exchange was likely incidental and forgettable. Yet, it was a turning point that would point Steve Jobs towards eastern philosophy."[3]

If our answers and reactions to questions people pose to us have the power to turn people toward or away from God, isn't it time to get serious about our answers? Isn't it time to learn what questions our fellow millennials are actually asking? What if we didn't slough off the tougher questions about God and our faith but instead engaged them? What if we took the questions and criticism of God and faith seriously and sought to help lead those asking the questions on

---

2   Walter Isaacson, *Steve Jobs* (New York: Simon and Schuster, 2015), 72-73.
3   Leadership Journal 33, no. 1 (Winter 2012), 20-23.

a journey towards God? We may struggle sometimes ourself and that's okay, because doubting is okay. Even Jesus allowed room for doubt.

This book you hold in your hands is the culmination of several answers to deep questions asked by myself and other millennials today. Upon moving into college ministry, I found many people had a genuine curiosity about Jesus Himself. What good is He really? If self-proclaimed "Christ-Followers" are so messed up, how good can Jesus really be? How is He any different than other religious figures? Why would it be good for me to follow Him and His way of life when there are other men and women I could follow as well? This book seeks to tackle those issues deeply, as well as handle other important spiritual inquiries. Too often those who profess to follow Jesus mar His image with their actions and reactions; their lack of Christ-like living only adds to the confusion for our generation. What good is Jesus really? This book tackles that answer; it will deal with how Jesus, among other ideologies and other gods, gives answers to a suffering world. This book will deal with Jesus as a holistic healer, a Savior, and much more.

You and I, whether we are a millennial or a leader of millennials, won't always have the answers, and we can't pretend that we do. But we must seek to find answers to the questions our fellow millennials ask to the best of our ability, because those asking are hungry for answers and hungry for truth—whether they would say that or not, they are. This hunger drives many in our generation down paths of destruction, but by simply taking time, we can walk through many of their questions, journeying with them. As we journey together, we must confront our own doubts and honestly share them. Skeptical or not, if you are a fellow millennial reading this, I hope you find answers to the questions you are asking.

If you are a leader of millennials, I hope you can use this book as a starting point to walk through the doubts and questions many of those you work with will have or are having. Millennials desire to be heard and answered. They are willing to sit and listen to the answers to their questions . . . and ask more along the way. This book seeks to attack those questions head-on and answer with both love and wisdom. You can use this book as a guide, a tool, a reference, or simply hand it to inquisitive young people to read through so they can have a resource to have with them.

If the answers given to our deep questions can lead us on the right path, let us begin that journey here together. May we honestly seek answers to the questions we have in life as to the goodness of Jesus. Whether or not you are skeptical about this journey, join me and learn how Jesus is good now and how He has always been good.

WHAT GOOD IS JESUS?

I'VE NOTICED A PATTERN AS I work with young adults and college students: they continuously desire to know what "good" or benefit something or someone will be or do for them. The question is no longer, "What is true?," but rather "What good is it?" Thus why I chose the title: "What Good Is Jesus?" This generation chooses many things based on how it benefits them. This is largely due to how consumeristic our society has become, and this is the society in which they've grown up. The world around this generation is constantly telling them that they need to find what's right for them and what is a best-fit scenario. This mantra gives them a sense of "testing" things out in order to see what is most beneficial to them, which results in this generation quite a bit of time to land anywhere. This testing has created a self-centered generation in many ways, causing this generation to make it about the experiences that can be received through the testing. Yet, due to our own subjectivity in the ways we test, I can't say it's all bad. The testing this generation does leads to many young adults actually dealing with certain issues as they crop up and spurs on moments of asking really good (and sometimes very difficult) questions. Not asking questions and blindly following people is a huge red flag to this current generation, so digging in deep and asking good questions is healthy, as is taking time to answer those questions. It can also turn into a "what's in it for me?" type of selfish mode of living, and, in many cases this has happened, those young people take a hodge-podge approach to spirituality and choose a bit of this faith and that faith to mash it into one that makes them feel comfortable. In this book we will see how Jesus is good in every area of a person's life and how He is the answer to their deep questions. Each chapter is based on certain questions I've dealt with in my own life and in ministry. The chapters wrestle with, in a relational way, the issues many young adults are wondering about.

JESUS IS PERSONAL AND CLOSE

MANY SOCIAL BEHAVIORAL EXPERTS HAVE gone on to share how Facebook is dangerous for our teens and young adults, causing them to have a distant, non-personal relationship with others, all while thinking they are connected. In this sense, I think we as an evangelical culture have had a "Facebook Official" relationship with Jesus much longer than Facebook has even existed. We teach that one must read the Bible and memorize the Scripture, believing that memorizing is actually what the Bible calls "putting God's Word in your heart." We teach that Christians must learn all they can about God, follow His commands, do the things He says to do, and avoid the things He says not to do. We teach and live a model of learning much about God, but rarely teach and live a life dedicated to seeking to truly *know Him*.

MOVING BEYOND JESUS' FACEBOOK PAGE

It is possible for me to creep all over people's Facebook page and learn all there is to know about them: who they like, don't like, shows they watch, books they read, where they often spend most of their time, what flavor of religion they're into, who their significant other is, and everything else. We can know almost everything there is to know about these people and still not understand the people themselves. Also, when thinking about Facebook, we post our stuff on there and usually choose to post the best stories, pictures, or notes about our current life. As someone said to me today, "We don't post selfies of us just waking up. We post the best pictures we've got!" I fear we do this with God as well—we portray the best of ourselves to the God of the Universe and pretend everything is okay when it really isn't. We are simply knowing "about" God, and we are portraying only our best to God, but we don't actually know each other at all—even though it looks like we know each other well.

This reality, my friends, is what many of us millennials are reacting against. We need to seek to experience the God of the Universe, not just educate our minds about Him. We need to seek a deep, rich, real, honest relationship with Him and not just be "Facebook Official" with Him. Many young people state they don't feel or experience God in church, so they seek to experience Him in many different (and sometimes wrong) places. Many in this current generation are really crying out for a personal God, not a distant one, yet many times we teach a very distant God.

Some people today are afraid of the words "experience God" because it seems as if we are lifting the "experience" above God; however, this isn't true at all. When I go to get coffee with a person, I don't have just a conversation; I am having a real-life experience of that person. I am experiencing this person's passions, personality, humor (or lack thereof), distastes, and manner of relating to me. We don't just meet people; we experience them. For too long, we've put the "knowing about God" above the knowing God. Reading the Bible, praying, and all of those things are GREAT. But if your faith is simply an educational task or a checklist of something you "should" do, then we've missed the point entirely and have hindered ourselves rather than helping ourselves. We've also built a false story about God, one that tells us we should simply be content knowing about Him rather than knowing Him for who He is. The generation we live in thrives on relationship, sometimes false relationships like Facebook, but that is the very reason we should be teaching the importance of truly *knowing* God.

God's word is "written on our hearts" when we naturally do what it says—not just blankly repeat it word for word. His Word is transformative as well as educational. It's not just something for our heads; it's for our very lives! This generation needs to see, meet, and speak to Jesus; God has given us His Spirit to be that very thing to this world.

Let us no longer perpetuate a Facebook relationship with Jesus, but rather, a real relationship. Rather than trying to do it all on our own, may we stop (as Brennan Manning calls it) "shoulding" on people but instead show them God by our actions, our love for one another, and our surrender to His power. Rachel Held Evans, on the CNN Belief Blog titled *Why Millennials are Leaving the Church* said:

> We want to be challenged to live lives of holiness, not only when it comes to sex, but also when it comes to living simply, caring for the poor and oppressed, pursuing reconciliation, engaging in creation care and becoming peacemakers.
>
> You can't hand us a latte and then go about business as usual and expect us to stick around. We're not leaving the church because we don't find the cool factor there; *we're leaving the church because we don't find Jesus there.*[4]

To me, that last phrase is her strongest point; they (we, because I am a millennial) don't see a lot of Jesus in the church. Instead of disciples of Jesus, who know Him and are known by Him, many of our churches are full of "Facebook Friends" of Jesus. I know as a lover of His Bride (the Church) that many Christians are well-intentioned and really desire to know God but are taught only how to be Facebook friends with Jesus and miss out on the deeper reality of actually experiencing Him.

When we see the Scriptures challenging us to do incredible things, knowing God and relying on His Spirit to empower us is truly the only way we can actually do any of it! So, let's shut down our Facebook accounts to Jesus and sit down and have a coffee with Him—so we can experience Him in real life! If Jesus is so good, what does knowing Him do?

THE ALMOST-CHRISTIAN CHURCH

In her book *Almost Christian*, Kenda Creasy Dean discusses her research studying and interviewing millennial Christian teenagers. She says that many teens are affected with a theological understanding of

---

4   Belief Blog; "Why Millennials are Leaving the Church," blog entry by Rachel Held Evans, July 27, 2013.

God labeled MTD, or Moralistic Therapeutic Deism, a term first coined by Christian Smith in *Soul Searching*. She states in her book, "Moralistic Therapeutic Deism is supplanting Christianity as the dominant religion in the United States."[5] In essence, MTD is the belief of many that God created, walked away, and His sole purpose of being "up there" is to monitor our good behavior and make us feel good when we need warm fuzzies. He is not close but distant. This, Dean states, makes these Christian teenagers *almost* Christian (or "Christian-ish"), but not quite. Another book written about this similar phenomenon, but for and about millennial young adults, is *Christian Atheist* by Craig Groschel, which shares similar ideas about how young adults tend to view God. This is a real issue in our generation.

Many of us may sometimes struggle with this idea of MTD. We don't always experience Jesus or know how to engage Him, so maybe He's distant. We wander through life asking what good is Jesus in this or that scenario, but we also get so bogged down with wondering this, that we ultimately ask the bigger question of "What good is Jesus?" in general. Is He good? If so, how?

As I was doing my daily devotional, *Know the Word* by John Soper[6], in week eleven, Tuesday's commentary struck me. So I changed everything I was looking to write and wrote this instead. The four main themes about God that Soper brought into thought what good God (and therefore Jesus) are boil down to four realities: He seeks, He speaks, He saves, and He sends. I'm taking Soper's four points of the goodness of Jesus and expounding upon them. The first one is about how He is seeking.

JESUS SEEKS TO BE PERSONALLY PRESENT WITH US

Behold, I stand at the door and knock. If anyone hears my voice and opens the door, I will come in to him and eat with him, and he with me (Rev. 3:20).

---

5   Kenda Creasy Dean, *Almost Christian: What the Faith of our Teens is Telling the American Church* (New York, Oxford University Press, 2010), 14.
6   See www.mission119.org for more information.

And the angel of the LORD appeared to him in a flame of fire out of the midst of a bush. He looked, and behold, the bush was burning, yet it was not consumed. And Moses said, "I will turn aside to see this great sight, why the bush is not burned." When the LORD saw that he turned aside to see, God called to him out of the bush, "Moses, Moses!" And he said, "Here I am." Then he said, "Do not come near; take your sandals off your feet, for the place on which you are standing is holy ground." And he said, "I am the God of your father, the God of Abraham, the God of Isaac, and the God of Jacob." And Moses hid his face, for he was afraid to look at God (Exod. 3:2-6).

God is not a distant God. He is the present, man-seeking God and has always been a God seeking for men to follow Him. He's not a whiney beggar following us around begging us to be with Him. He is, however, a lover seeking to give His love to all of mankind. Jesus then, being God, seeks to be personally present with us. He desires not only a simple, communal connection with us, but also a personal one where we speak to Him, and He with us, on a deep, real, honest, and individual level. Jesus says: "Behold, I stand at the door and knock." It's a simple statement within a letter to the church in Laodicea who were too interested in themselves and their stuff to pay attention to God.

Yet, here we see Jesus stating to them that He is seeking after them. He is looking for them and is at their very door knocking. He was declaring to them His desire to be present with them! William Barclay, a world-renowned scholar and commentator says this: "The unique new fact that Christianity brought into this world is that God is the one who seeks for people. No other religion has the vision of a seeking God."[7] This idea was a new concept for many. Being familiar with the story of Moses having a face-to-face relationship with God shouldn't have been a new concept to the Jews because God met Moses

---

7   William Barclay, *The New Daily Study Bible: The Revelation of John* (Louisville: Westminster John Knox Press, 2004), 160.

face-to-face. In the story of Moses, we see God seeking out Moses. Forty years prior to God seeking Moses, we see Moses fleeing for his life into the wilderness away from Egypt with his people, the Israelites. We see no indication of Moses seeking after God; in fact, he may have been running from God for the past forty years. Yet in this passage we see God seeking Moses out and finding him in the middle of nowhere. Here we see God Himself being present with Moses. Genesis also tells the story of a seeking God. After Adam and Eve sinned, God comes into the Garden and asks: "Where are you?" God desires to transform our lives by sharing with us just how desirous of us He is. No other religion talks about a God who seeks. Jesus is unique in His coming to us. We simply have to let Him through the door of our lives. Christ will never break in; He must be invited in. Jesus is not just seeking and present, but when we invite Him in, He is a speaking God as well.

JESUS SPEAKS WITH HIS BRIDE

Jesus stated in Revelation 3:20: "I will come in to him and eat with him, and he with me." This passage may not seem very "conversational," but we may not understand it as His original audience would have. At the time Revelation was written, there were three main meals many people (especially the Greeks) would eat. Breakfast, which was a quickly eaten meal of dried bread dipped in wine, and then a midday meal, which was also a short, non-exciting meal. But then came dinner, or *deipnon* as it is said in the Greek. This was the evening meal, the main meal of the day, and people lingered over this meal. The day's work was behind them, and they could fellowship, laugh, and talk.[8] Here Jesus says if you open the door I knock on, I will have *deipnon* with you. Jesus desires to have conversations with us that last for hours. Imagine, the King of the Universe desiring to have a long-lasting, lingering meal with you. Here, He is declaring that to us. Jesus is good because He desires this deep intimacy. No other god declares such a desire. We also see that this was God's way all along.

---

8   Concept for this comes in: William Barclay, *The New Daily Study Bible: The Revelation of John* (Louisville: Westminster John Knox Press, 2004), 161.

In the story of Moses, God talks directly to him as a friend would have—face-to-face. This is a constant theme in the life of Moses, and because of Jesus' death and resurrection, we too can have this type of intimacy with God, sitting in His presence. This is the understanding that the great saints of the past and present understand. We ask how can they do what they do? How can they believe the way they do? How can they see the miracles and healings they get to see? The saints got this idea: Jesus' presence shifts the atmosphere of our lives. This is why A.W. Tozer says, "Wherever faith has been original, wherever it has proved itself to be real, it has invariably had upon it a sense of the present God."[9] This message isn't just for people who are "non-believers," but it's also for us who say we believe. Jesus desires *deipnon* with you. When's the last time you invited Him into a deep, real, raw area of your life and spent time lingering in fellowship with him? He desires to be present and to have His presence in your life to be transformative.

JESUS SAVES THE LOST

Jesus declares in Luke 19:10 His purpose for being on the earth, to seek and save the lost. He was and is a rescuer. He is the ultimate deliverer of people. Moses was a micro deliverer, and Jesus is the macro deliverer. When we look at the Scripture, we must remember that every arrow points towards Jesus. Jesus is essentially on every page of the Bible, both Old and New testaments. So, in this passage of Luke, Jesus echoes what was said in the burning bush to Moses: "I have come down to deliver them." The Israelites were lost in their persecution. They were stuck in their slavery and needed a deliverer. Jesus is good because He came to deliver us from our sin and save us. In this salvation too is a cleansing. 1 John 1:7 states: "The blood of Jesus His Son cleanses us from all sin."

Every time I now hear the phrase "cleanses us from all sin," I have a story of my son that comes to mind. It was a regular evening when my wife Hilary and I tucked the kids into bed, but my son MJ declared

---

9   A.W. Tozer, *God's Pursuit of Man* (Chicago: Moody Press), 7.

he was having severe stomach troubles. He did this often, so we gave him a drink of water and a cheese stick (his normal go-to hungry food), and he seemed fine. Roughly an hour or so later, we hear him screaming that he had vomited. I run into the room because Hilary has a very sensitive gag reflex and can't handle the smell or look of puke without vomiting herself.

I see my little man covered in his own vomit, so I decide to strip him down and bathe him. He fought with me for a while, but eventually he conceded. After he was bathed and redressed, he vomited again, and it was everywhere. I redo the process I just finished and clean him in the bath. I also had to wipe down the floor and myself. Once he was back in his bed, he began to wail in pain and shout how badly his stomach was bothering him. I decided to put him in bed with Hilary and me after he fussed for so long about not being able to get back to sleep due to his continuing stomach pains. His stomach was so bad that he ended up pooping in his pants—in our bed. So once again, I placed him in the bathtub where he again had some more vomit. I cleaned him again and told him how much I loved him and how sorry I was for him being sick. I didn't find myself angry with my son for all of the craziness he brought forward. I simply had a deep-rooted compassion to clean this poor boy of all of his mess. Once he allowed me to clean him and stopped fighting the bath, it became much easier for me to clean him. No matter how many times he puked or pooped, I was willing to cleanse his body.

I truly believe this is how Jesus feels about delivering and cleansing us. His mission to save us was to deliver us from our mess. We may not even know how much spiritual vomit we have on ourselves, but He does, and His heart's desire is to cleanse us from all of it. Jesus is good because He seeks, He speaks, He saves, and He sends.

JESUS SENDS HIS BRIDE TO THE WORLD
(MATT. 28:19-20; EXOD. 3:10)

Jesus sends those who understand His Goodness into the world to continue to cultivate this knowing of Himself. When we "get it" He sends us out to spread this amazing news of a seeking, speaking, saving Deliverer. He sent Moses to Pharaoh and sent Jesus to earth and Jesus now sends His bride into the world. When we truly grasp the depth of how good Jesus is, we will desire to live differently, being transformed by His presence in our lives, and we will desire for others to experience this seeking, speaking, and saving God. When we capture His fullness and are infused with His Spirit, this "being sent" will continue to come naturally to us, and we will begin to see every moment as being sent. Jesus didn't commute to earth; He lived here. Being sent doesn't mean we pick and choose when we are sent; it means our lives are to be lived as one sent.

Have you experienced the full goodness of Jesus in His seeking, speaking, saving, and sending? If not, where are you missing something He has for you? He deeply desires to be known by us, may we pursue knowing Him.

REFLECTIONS ON "JESUS IS PERSONAL AND CLOSE"

1. How have you (if you have) experienced the presence of Jesus in your life?

2. What does it mean to you that Jesus is good because He seeks, speaks, saves, and sends?

3. What importance is it that Jesus, the King of the Universe desires to be a personal and close part of your life?

JESUS HAS A PURPOSE FOR HUMANITY

WE LIVE IN A WORLD that wants to know what things in life are good for them and at the same time for the whole of humanity. We find ourselves in a pluralistic society that is deeply humanistic and desires to be a people that reach out to help our fellow man. This desire is especially more prevalent with the emerging generations. This generation's heart is to know which things add good to the world and to their own life. They see people clinging to religious perspectives, but ask, "Why do these things really matter in the scheme of real life?" If people of this generation can't find the answer to that question, they easily discard the whole thing. A prominent question that I've heard asked in several different ways is: "Does Jesus have a purpose for humanity?" In this question is a need to connect an ethereal deity to everyday life. Much of what is "religious" is a deeper experience that is set in motion for people to conform to a certain way of living or lifestyle. If Jesus is simply good so that the "church" enforces the conformity Jesus "required," then He is not the deity for this generation.

However, Jesus is not about conformity. In fact, in many areas in the Gospels we see that He rejects certain areas of conformity within the Jewish culture that arose or were arising. He bucked the system and challenged those areas of conformity in some pretty harsh ways. Jesus has a purpose for humanity beyond conformity!

Sadly, many unsaved people have a picture of Christians (and subsequently, Jesus) that has been largely controlled by the media and a few ridiculous zealots in our country. This particular picture paints the idea that there is little to no good in Jesus' followers, and if the followers of this good teacher act in a way that seems less humane or less caring than others of different life perspectives, it leaves little to no desire to be like them or to follow whom they follow. This negative view of Christians makes the good teacher no longer labeled "good" because when His followers publicly display their lack of goodness in His name, they then are giving Him a bad reputation. With these pictures and images of "Christ followers," Jesus' reputation has been besmirched, and He's made out to be something that is entirely different than who He truly is. The imagery of much of current Christianity is painted simply as a religion of conformity. This painting puts together a mosaic where there seems to be little respect or tolerance for the human condition or human brokenness and depicts this movement of Jesus as a bunch of pharisaical zealots. These zealots then are not out to save people from hell but to cause them to be conformed to a certain set of rules and doctrine, which is not life-giving at all. Christianity then, rather than being life-giving, seems life-draining. Working in our own strength to do the right thing and treating poorly those who fail to do so causes people to walk away.

THE CONFORMING GOSPEL?

When studying current culture, hearing modern language and attitudes towards the followers of Jesus, one quickly comes to the conclusion that His followers are separatists who care little for anyone else and are globally ignorant of the devastation, pain, and harsh realities going on in our world. Many of these followers have been publicly quoted as calling some inhumane happenings "God's judgment" on sinners. Others appear to have no heart for the poverty, pain, and brokenness of the world around us. Their selfishness seems to be especially true for mega-churches that appear to be slick, all-white, rich people who care more about their domain and their dominance in society rather than their fellow man who needs help. As a follower of Christ, I must admit that sadly, in my personal experience, this has been true for a large portion of Western Christians. I must highlight the word *Western* in that statement because other Christ-followers in different parts of the world do not fall into this ignorance as much as we in America and in England do.

I must confess that, in my own life, I have fallen into this trap of being concerned for myself and for the conformity of those around me. I am not naturally philanthropic in my life at all and am naturally selfish. I am a person who looks out for himself and desires to take care of myself above all others. I was not a person deeply affected by world tragedies, and instead of seeing them as something I needed to help out with, I saw them as annoying news clips that I had to suffer through. As I write that, I hate my words, but I know them to be true. I was not living a life outside of the normal "media perception" of the religion of which I was a part.

In order for us to walk together on this journey to discover what good Jesus is, and in particular why Jesus has a purpose for humanity that is good, I must be open and honest with you as to who I was and show you who I am now. If I am not honest with you, I have done you wrong and would have perverted this journey. My hope is that by being open as I write, your guard will come down, which will spur an honest reflection of yourself. Whether you consider yourself Christian or not, introspection is always needed.

I cared very little for global issues and helped very little in them. I hate that this is true, not only for myself, but also for a majority of Western Christians. This hasn't always been the case. Many of the relief organizations started from a Christian's desire to help those in need. The American Red Cross and The Salvation Army come to mind among those relief organizations that have strong Christian roots. However, many Western Christians find themselves on the sidelines of global issues, or if they get involved, these Christians simply send money without being actively involved with their time.

CORRECTLY REFLECTING GOD'S IMAGE

When the people who claim to know God don't care for the world as a whole, their actions cause those watching to wonder if God actually has a purpose for humanity. If all Christians were to sit on the sidelines during a global crisis (which all would not, but for the sake of this conversation imagine this scenario), then we would have to conclude that the pain happening in those situations doesn't move their God. Christians are called "the image of God," so whether we like it or not, our actions reflect (for good or ill) the God we serve.

The reality is that there are stories the media can finagle in order to match the world's perceived reality on Christians caring for global issues (or lack thereof), but there are also true stories of Christians in this world that need no finagling. These stories are just plain, sad testaments to a lack of care for the globe as a whole.

What good is Jesus?

Does He care for humanity or simply His own interests?

Is He all about conformity to a lifestyle, or something far deeper?

What kind of response would Jesus urge His followers to have when crisis hits the world or those hurting?

JESUS CARES ABOUT HUMANITY

When one looks at the life of Jesus, we can see His deep, true, honest, and opulent care for humanity. We see a man, who says He is God loving on the down and out, caring for those who are hurting. We see Jesus wracked with pain over a friend's death. We see Jesus caring little for Himself and His personal interests and looking out for others and their needs. His life, as listed in all of the Gospels, speaks to His heart for the lost and the broken. All one needs to do is read even a small portion of these books of the Bible to catch a glimpse of the heart of Jesus, and ultimately the heart of God the Father.

Jesus was a God/Man on a mission; don't misunderstand what I'm saying. He knew why He was here and lived His life with utter strength and purpose set to the goal (Luke 19:10). He, however, didn't ignore those He found hurting along the way. He didn't let His mission overtake His desire to care for humanity on His way to the cross. His driven-ness didn't give Him an out to ignore the pain of the leper or the hurt of the woman caught in adultery. In fact, His mission and His endgame pushed Him to care, love, and serve. He was setting an example for His followers, showing them that they must do as He did. Jesus knew that the "religious" people thought they had it made in the shade when it came to eternity with God. Jesus attempted several times to point out to these religious leaders that they simply "thought" they were righteous. They, however, missed His point and instead killed Him for suggesting they had any issues to work out. I believe we have many people living today who may feel as if they are guaranteed a spot next to Jesus as well due to their "piety" and "righteous" lives. It is many of these types of people that sadly define Jesus and His followers to the world and cause those looking on to wonder if Jesus even had an actual plan or desire for humanity.

We all have the option of admitting our problems and getting healthy, or ignoring them and staying deathly ill and thinking we are good (like the Pharisees). Jesus desires us to own up to our wounds, not ignore them (Matt. 11:28-29). He would desire that His followers respond with care, love, and empathy—not despondence, ignorance, or apathy. Someone once said that the opposite of love isn't hate but apathy, and I think Jesus would agree with such a statement. Jesus was a deep lover of people and worked to open the eyes of the blind in the physical as well as the spiritual sense. He desires His followers to exude the same type of love and desire for the world that He did.

LIVING AS RESTORERS

If Jesus cares for humanity and calls His followers to take the same care, what are His followers doing to effect positive change in our world?

This is the common question that comes within the conclusion that Christ cares for humanity. So many things have been said against the followers of Jesus that make one think that most followers lack in their caring for humanity. Are there lackadaisical Christians who care not for their fellow man? Yes. However, there is a new wave of young believers who Gabe Lyons, in his book *Next Christians,* labels the "Restorers." These young believers are on the move to reunite the Jesus who cares with the followers who care. Restorers deeply care for humanity and truly desire to restore those who are broken, both physically and spiritually.

One story of restoration is that of Allegheny Center Alliance Church in Pittsburgh, PA. Rock and Karen Dillaman came to this church with a heart to serve the community. They loved, cared, and worked with the people of the community, and their ministry grew into a large church. The Dillamans' story deeply moved leaders who desired to make serving people more important than staying huddled up in a bubble of like-minded people. Rock, the Lead Pastor is no sepa-ratist; he is a Restorer. Pittsburgh was, and still is, a hurting community, and, by the example of Jesus and the empowerment of His Holy Spirit, this church has begun and sustained for many years a restorative hope within the city. Living like Jesus lived and simply serving those who needed served sparked a huge movement that even the mayor recog-nized as significant. I am proud to be a part of such a church!

The Dillamans are just one example of Jesus' followers dishing out the love of humanity that Jesus did. What are we doing for the world? Where can we take a page out of Jesus' book and really throw ourselves into the heart of Jesus' love for this world?

When asked that question, a friend of mine answered back strongly with his own desire to follow Christ's passion for those in need. Chris Coakley, a youth pastor in Ohio, had a passion to connect his teens to a global movement. So during a thirty-hour famine-type event[10], he dedicated himself to raising funds to purchase food for those in Burkina Faso and Gabon who needed it. Chris had connections with missionaries on the ground in these countries and knew that they would get the food delivered to the people in need. His youth group raised a lot of money, and Chris felt called to continue this project. He

---

10   www.30hourfamine.org

has now started a non-profit organization called Grain of Hope 58:10[11], and he is raising money for food and water for those in need in Gabon and Burkina Faso. What is even more astounding is that 100% of the money goes directly to these efforts! Chris is passionate about restoring those hurting in Africa and is a lover of people, just like his Savior. It is a remarkable story he has to tell and God has surely grabbed his heart for the things that matter. In fact, the verse that sparked all of this for Chris, the verse that asked him that tough question of "What are you going to do?" was Isaiah 58:10, which says:

If you pour yourself out for the hungry and satisfy the desire of the afflicted, then shall your light rise in the darkness and your gloom be as the noonday.

That verse shows the heart of God who pours Himself out for the hungry and satisfies the desires of the afflicted. Jesus also deeply desires that His followers do the very same.

Many unbelievers who come to see Christ and a select few of His followers really caring about the world also end up hearing that Jesus is God. The next train of thought for this group is then to question Jesus' goodness. If He is good, how can He allow bad things to happen? How can this loving, caring Jesus be a God who allows destruction, pain, and hurt to even happen? Many ask if He is willing to help them through the pain, why doesn't He just make sure the pain doesn't even happen in the first place? If I am honest, my work with the younger generations has shown me that this is one of the most often asked questions. I share with them these stories of Jesus caring for the world, stories of Jesus being God, and stories of Rock and Chris. But people always ask the same question: then why does bad stuff happen?

TRUE LOVE IS NOT FORCED

God did not create humans as robots. He designed us to think and act as we so desired. If He had made you obey His commands, giving you no choice in your design, would you be able to understand love?

---

11   Go to www.grainofhope.org to find out more about this awesome ministry!

Or would your obedience be forced? God loved us enough to let us choose His way or not His way. Sadly, many humans choose against the way of God, as did Adam and Eve in the beginning (Gen. 3). When that sin occurred, it caused something to be attached to humans at birth, namely the sin nature. Suffering happens as a result (mostly) of sin (we will dig much deeper into suffering later). God *can* force us to do His will, but then we would have no understanding of love. Suffering is bad, but without suffering and choices, we would simply be robots commanded from on high. Remember, Jesus Himself suffered as we do:

> For we do not have a high priest who is unable to sympathize with our weaknesses, but one who in every respect has been tempted as we are, yet without sin (Heb. 4:15; more on this verse later).

God can also use suffering to shape and mold us into better people.

> Count it all joy, my brothers, when you meet trials of various kinds, for you know that the testing of your faith produces steadfastness. And let steadfastness have its full effect, that you may be perfect and complete, lacking in nothing (James 1:2-4).

I have experienced a lot of suffering in my life. I will go into the details of my suffering in the next chapter, but I have seen my fair share. We see story after story in the Bible of suffering and how God used it to grow people. I'm sure you as well have experienced suffering and have a whole host of stories of your suffering to contribute. All of us have experienced suffering to some degree or another.

Christ came and died the most horrible death to save us from sin and eternal death. He suffered worse than anyone probably will ever suffer. He suffered for you and for me. When we have hard times, God is there to lean on. He will get us through; our suffering is not in vain! We have the hope of resurrection. Let me finish this question with a quote and a question from C.S. Lewis: "They say of some temporal suffering 'No future bliss can make up for it,' not knowing that Heaven, once attained, will work backwards and turn even that agony into glory."[12] If there were no suffering and life were perfect, would we ever turn to God?

JESUS HAS A HOLISTIC VIEW OF PURPOSE

Jesus cares more deeply for humanity than anyone else who will ever live or who has ever lived, but He also cares about more than doing good to the least of these. Jesus' heart not only helps and heals the broken, but brings *spiritual* wholeness to people as well. For all of us, it's easy to see the physical pain of this world, but harder to see the spiritual pain of those around us. Many in our world care about the current reality with too little thought to the eternal reality. Sadly, many Christians have the opposite problem. A good number of Christians think too much about the eternal reality and think too little on the current reality. This eternal focus causes the people of the world to miss the truth of the Gospel. Those who are entrusted to live out the Gospel are abdicating that in order to remain in holy huddles. Instead of blessing the world, they ignore it. Many people need to see that Jesus cares about them now as they are in their physical or emotional brokenness. In many cases Jesus attacks both issues at the same time—spiritual brokenness (due to sin) as well as emotional or physical brokenness (i.e. the woman caught in adultery as explained below and the man lowered through the roof). In order for a Christian in today's culture to gain a voice in the spiritual brokenness, they must first approach the physical and/or emotional brokenness.

Jesus desires that we not only cover the earthly wound with bandages and help the world to heal from those wounds, but also expose the spiritual wounds that are there and show the world how to be healed eternally. There are emotional and spiritual wounds that people in our world deal with on a daily basis. If anyone in this world were to

---

12   C.S. Lewis, *Christian Reflections* (Grand Rapids: Wm. B. Eerdmans Publishing Co., 2014), 155.

say they have no deep scarring, this person is lying. Everyone has scars. Jesus desires to heal those deep wounds. In John 8, Jesus does this for a woman. The Pharisees wanted to trap Jesus into doing something wrong, so they devised a plan to catch a particular woman in the act of adultery. This whole scenario on the part of the Pharisees seemed ludicrous because it was a setup, not only for Jesus, but for this woman as well. In my opinion, the only way I can see how they actually pulled this off is that they had some guy convince this woman to sleep with him, which then is condoning sex outside of marriage. I imagine that they told the guy they hand-picked to have a "free pass" and have sex; all he had to do is tell them the place and time of where he'll be having sex with this woman. The Pharisees will then overlook the man's sexual sin in order to drag the woman in all her shame before Jesus to force Jesus to make a decision on the matter concerning the woman's sexual sins in a public arena. The Pharisees are giving this guy the freedom to sin, so they can trap Jesus in sin. It's ridiculous, and what really stinks for them is, it fails.

The Pharisees bring this woman who was "caught in the act of adultery" before Jesus to hear what His judgment upon her will be. They are pointing fingers, accusing this woman, yelling at her, calling her horrible names, and Jesus remains silent and doodles in the sand. This woman has been beaten down by religion and road-torn by the streets of life. She's probably poor. She is definitely broken, now she lies on the ground half-naked in shame for all to see. Most religious people (Christians included) would love to point the finger at this woman and spit nasty names her way, but not Jesus. Jesus reaches out and loves her. He stands up to her accusers and shoos them away by stating those without sin can go ahead and kill her.

Jesus doesn't leave it there, however, because He cares about more than just the surface problems of humanity. He cares about the emotional and spiritual problems of humanity. He picks the woman up and asks her where her accusers are, which begins to heal her emotional problem. He then says something rather odd: "Now go and sin no more," which heals her spiritual problem. Jesus has a purpose for humanity. His purpose is far deeper than any other religious figure could ever dream up. His purpose for humanity is to be *restored*, not destroyed, not thrown out, but to be restored—*fully* restored.

We've looked at how we humans are to blame for the chaos in this world, not God. We are the ones who chose this world to be broken, not Jesus. Jesus hates what this world has become just as much as we do. His heart is broken for the poor. His heart is broken for the dying children in remote countries. His heart aches for AIDS victims. His mind worries over the homeless. He desperately longs for restoration to happen. He deeply desires us to turn from the fallen nature and brokenness of this world and to be healed in this life and the next. His desire is that once we are fully restored, we can then be the hands and feet of His restoration project.

For too long, generations of Christians have missed their role in this process. For too long, I have missed my role in this process. Let it be so no more! Jesus has a purpose for humanity, and His purpose is the heart cry of this generation: real, authentic living that brings positive change for all humanity. This world is seeking desperately after a purpose for humanity. Why are we here? What is the reason for my life? Is it all to live and die, or is there a greater meaning to it all?

JESUS AMONG OTHER FIGURES

When we compare Jesus to other religious leaders or even other religions, they fall massively short of the bar Jesus sets for humanity and His intention for restoring humanity. Many think that Jesus' followers have ruined the true meaning of Christ's life, and to some degree they are right. But Jesus, when looked at as He is and not taking into account some current feelings about His followers, is purely motivated by love for the world. Other religious figures had no such raw depth of care for humanity to them as Jesus has. Most religious efforts are selfishly motivated, seeking the best life for yourself by doing X, Y, and Z. Love the poor because it will help you. Find your chi so you can connect to the great gods and ancestors of the past, present, and future. Take care of the environment, or the "Great Mother" will wipe you out. You must do good works to earn Allah's affections. At their core, these religions serve as selfish motivators for good deeds. Jesus is different. Once we meet Him, experience Him, feel Him, love Him, and decide to follow Him, we simply desire to do good works. We know deep down that we are just as broken as the ones we serve; yet Christ brought us out of that pit. Inside, we know that God deeply loves the people we serve, so we love them.

Atheism and the Big Bang theory of creation, at their core beliefs, leave humans without any purpose. If we are all accidents after all, who cares if a few die off? Shouldn't we control the population through genocide and abortions? Shouldn't we then live for our own happiness, rather than that of others? The idea of humans serving humans flies in the face of survival of the fittest. In fact, those who are strongest should be overpowering the weak. We shouldn't care, according to evolution, about speaking about the poor, or the beaten down. Yet we do. Why? Because deep down, we believe that there must be purpose for humanity, all of humanity, not just a select few. In our core, it doesn't sit well to *not* have compassion. We make purpose even out of a system that refutes purpose.

The world is asking good questions, yet it finds conclusions in the wrong places. Christians must live lives that show Jesus is the way. Christians need to be living like Jesus lived and showing this world that God truly does have a purpose for humanity. He desires for it to be restored. Other gods, no matter how good their followers are, do not have such a purpose for humanity.

Every god that is not *the* God requires that we do stuff for him or her in order to gain his or her love. Allah demands you live a good life. Buddha demands you find your inner peace and don't slip into certain emotions. For gods like these, and other religions, the gods are angry gods who must always be made happy. The God of the Bible is a God of love who is the *only* God in all religions who sacrificed Himself so that we can be made right with Him. He loves us for who we are and loves us enough not to let us stay that way.

All other gods won't love you until you get right and act right. Also, the other "great founders" of other religions have graves. Our God is the only resurrected God! All others have marked graves and tombs where they died and never rose again. Jesus says in John 14:6, "I am the way, and the truth, and the life. No one comes to the Father except through me." He also said, "I am the resurrection and the life. Whoever believes in me, though he die, yet shall he live, and everyone who lives and believes in me shall never die. Do you believe this?" (John 11:25-26).

Five hundred people saw Jesus after He rose from the dead (1 Cor. 15:6). He said He was God and because we know this was true, we must stand by it. If Jesus is God (which He proved He is by His resurrection) and Jesus said He is the only way, we must conclude and have faith that He is the only way. Not all roads lead to God; every other path worships a different god, who has a different purpose for humanity than Jesus does.

WHAT GOOD IS JESUS THEN?

Jesus is the only good for humanity. His desire, unlike all others, is to give purpose to humanity. He lived His life as a servant (Phil. 2) to show His love for humanity. He died a death so great, so inhumane as to save humanity from being lost. Some people would combat this idea of eternal salvation with weird ideas that are so attractive, many believe them. People, even within the church, refute the idea that without Christ, the afterlife would be a literal hell. The Scriptures talk about Jesus saving us, and it wasn't just from this life. Jesus is good because He sacrificed Himself, one Friday, for all of humanity (1 John 2:2). Once we understand His sacrifice, we have to trust His death and believe His purpose for our life is the only purpose for life. When you look at His life and the statements He made, it is easy to see He is good because He truly cared for and desired restoration of humanity.

REFLECTIONS ON "JESUS HAS A PURPOSE FOR HUMANITY"

1. How does Atheism/Evolution break down to purposeless life?

2. What are your thoughts/reactions to why we suffer?

3. What pain in your life has God brought you through, that you can say now has a purpose?

JESUS UNDERSTANDS OUR SUFFERING

SUFFERING IN THIS LIFE IS inescapable; it is all around us, and the pain of suffering is the sure thing every human can commiserate on together. Even if that pain from one person to the next is different, pain is still pain, and we can come together and have long-into-the-night discussions about the things that have brought us suffering. Many people today and in history can connect due to similar types of suffering and grow stronger as they share their stories together. Meetings like Alcoholics Anonymous are strong because it is a sure-fire formula for success; their issues, struggles, and suffering are so similar that people connect, realize they are not the only ones, and find this place to be safe for them to be completely open and honest with their pain.

PRETENDING TO BE FINE WHEN WE'RE NOT

If you live and breathe you will experience suffering and will endure pains of many shapes and sizes; that thought is pretty depressing, but true. Sadly, for most of my life, I kept my burdens of my suffering and pains hidden, locked up and secret—even from myself. This hiddenness affected the way I lived, the way I interacted with others, and caused so much confusion that I found myself adding to my pain by slipping into a short addiction to pornography in high school and the beginning of college. I knew I had deep pains in my past, but I assumed the majority of those things were long dead and buried; however, I realized that much of that deep pain was simply placed in a shallow grave that was easily accessible and, when accessed, caused me to shove it down further and further by way of my new-found addiction. My problem, in large part, was that I had become so accustomed to ignoring my pain that I didn't even realize it was there. When symptoms of the bigger problem like pornography entered the picture, I was sure I was the only one struggling with such a grievous, heinous sin—so I kept it all quiet. It was a great coping mechanism to avoid realizing my deeper issues of the soul, that in fact the suffering of pain and loss I had previously experienced and thought were gone were not gone at all, but clawing their way into my inner life.

Lies swirled within me that no one would understand, everyone would be against me, and I would be judged, mocked, and denied access to God because of my addiction to pornography. I didn't fully grasp the true fact that Jesus actually could understand my pain and could understand my suffering. I grew up in church hearing how perfect He was and how He thwarted Satan and the demonic temptations Satan brought towards Him. What a victor Jesus was and what a scumbag I turned out to be, so unlike this mighty hero of the Biblical narrative. I began to live with this identity and the lies grew bigger and bigger within my heart. I had developed a second, false self due to my pain, and I was certain Jesus wouldn't understand.

HOW CAN JESUS UNDERSTAND?

How could Jesus understand my parents' divorce? His parents weren't divorced like mine were; He grew up in a nice, intact family, right? His parents both said "yes" to God about His being born, and they saw the miracles that happened due to their choice. How could Jesus begin to understand my personal issues of sin and suffering?

How could Jesus understand that I was ripped from all I knew, that the family I had was in shambles, and I was now living as a drifting loner who lived with a drunken step-dad? How could Jesus understand the pain of loss where I was rejected by my mother and saw my father attempt suicide? How could Jesus understand the life-changing effects of moving from one parent to the next, moving cities, churches, and everything . . . again? How could Jesus understand leaving my siblings behind and feeling a gaping hole in my life for not living in the same house as them?

When it came down to it, I didn't actually believe that He did understand or that He even could. The Jesus I grew up knowing was a tame and quiet goody-goody. The Jesus I was taught about died for my sins and was a perfect angel. The Jesus I heard about would reject sinners with baggage like mine—at least the way He was portrayed to me left me feeling this way. He was not a safe haven, nor was He a "harbor in the storm;" He was a judgmental, perfect pretty boy who wouldn't care about my pain. He'd only make it worse. Yeah, He died for my sins, but if I messed up after I came clean the first time, I was no longer "fit to be in His Kingdom." These were all perceived ideas of Jesus I had formed, not by the teachings I received but by the Christians I interacted with; the way they lived their lives with duplicity taught me that I too needed to live duplicitously.

Those thoughts were buried deep within me, because I went to college to be a pastor. I couldn't even be honest about how I felt about Jesus—not even to myself. The scary thing about this whole scenario is I fooled myself into thinking that I actually was fine, that I had no problems. I told myself that if I would just be a good Christian boy, on the outside at least, and made Jesus and all my superiors happy, I would be the best pastor the church had seen in a long while. I prided myself on how together I was, how religious I was, and how much I loved Jesus. I was eager to prove my worth to my professors, to prove my abilities to my classmates (as well as rub in how awesome I am to them in the process), and to make everyone happy if I could.

In short, I was living a lie, and it all stemmed from my untapped, unhealed pain that I kept secret; it also stemmed from my deep denial of Jesus' ability to do anything about it. I was truly and wholly lost, but I thought I was completely fine. I was a walking Pharisee and was super proud of it, and no one could tell me differently.

No one that is, until I began to realize I wasn't fine. I had a long stretch of many days in a row, up to multiple times a day that I turned to pornography for solace and I realized something within me truly was broken. I thought, "I can't keep this a secret for much longer, maybe I need some help." Of course, shortly after feeling this, my old beliefs about the judgmental Jesus sprung back up, and I believed it unsafe to admit my problem, much less the deeper realities of my secret pain. Soon, I would realize that my hidden, secret assumptions about Jesus were dead wrong, but for that moment they still held sway over my heart like a vice grip sucking the life out of me slowly but surely.

HOW I REALIZED JESUS REALLY DID
UNDERSTAND MY SUFFERING AND PAIN

It wasn't just a moment, but a progression of moments that awakened my heart to the stark realities that Jesus really did understand my pain. Usually I find the best processes are the ones that happen gradually over time, and that is how it happened with me. I was rudely awakened to my own false piety in college, where many people pointed out my arrogance and called me to live differently. I had covered up my pain that I couldn't really feel much of anything anymore, except feeling good about my religiosity. I slowly found myself around people who were closer to the Spirit of God than any others I had ever met, and they spoke hard truth into my life. Although the words were hard, they were good and healthy for me to hear. I learned the truth from Proverbs 27:6a that states: "Faithful are the wounds of a friend."

I remember clear as day when my mentor asked me this question: "Marvin, do you want to be a great pastor or just a good one?" I knew the answer and so did he; I already was great! He then blew me away sharing how if I desired to be great I needed to go to counseling. Of course I wrestled with this for a long time but then came to the conclusion that maybe this would be good after all (with the loving push of my father and now wife). This was the beginning of my journey to understanding that Jesus really did understand what I was going through.

When it comes to our pain and Jesus there are generally three main camps. 1) Those who believe that Jesus understands their pain. 2) Those who don't trust that He understands their pain and, as a result, reject Him. 3) Those who don't trust He understands, and cover their pain through religious works for Him. I was clearly in camp #3 but thought I was in camp #1. Counseling and a spiritual awakening revealed my true nature: I was a hot mess full of pain and agony. Here in my journey, I finally admitted my deep-rooted pains and losses, pain I had long since written off and dutifully gave testimony about. Yet it was still there because of a firm belief within myself that Jesus couldn't, and wouldn't, understand.

It was then, at the peak of my vulnerability that I saw Jesus' story truly for the first time. I saw in Hebrews 4:15 where the author of that book states: "For we do not have a high priest who is unable to sympathize with our weaknesses, but one who in every respect has been tempted as we are, yet without sin." As a good Christian (wink, wink), I had read this passage before, but something in me now understood this at a deeper level. I was able to read it this way: "Marvin, I know your pain. I know your suffering. I can sympathize because I too have experienced your pain: rejection, loneliness, betrayal, humiliation, and loss. Take a look at my story again, this time with open eyes, looking for where I've experienced your pain." It was then that I re-started a new journey of understanding Jesus, looking into the Gospels and finding my heart burdened with this enormous reality that Jesus really did walk through my pain. He experienced rejection almost every day of His life, and when His disciples deserted Him on the Mount of Olives, He was left to face everything Good Friday had to offer, all without any human comfort.

JESUS WALKED THROUGH SIMILAR SUFFERING AS WE HAVE

He lost friends, gained enemies each time He stepped into a city, and was stabbed in the back by one of His closest friends and disciples. His story, although filled with power, healing, and amazing ministry, was also filled with many sorrows. This doesn't even include the reality of His horrific death and the physical pain that it brought about. I knew *about* these parts of His story and knew about these pains, but I didn't *know* how it pertained to me. These parts of Jesus' story were sad to me, but it never clicked that because of these, Jesus really could understand and even relate to my pains and wounds. He was familiar with them because *they were His own*!

When you look through the Gospels to seek when and where Jesus' pain relates to yours, you can't help but feel the powerful reality that your pains and wounds are understood. In his book *God's Favorite Place on Earth*, Frank Viola says: "The Lord is able to comfort you because He knows exactly what you're going through. He understands your pain, having been there Himself. So we can rest our heads on a God who knows what it feels like firsthand."[13]

Frank here points to the deeper issue, which is not simply that Jesus understands what we've been through, but also the need for comfort and healing to take place within us. When a friend commiserates with me in my suffering it's nice to know I am not alone, but that doesn't do much for healing those deep wounds. There has to be something more to it than simply His understanding, and Jesus not only understands our pain but also can comfort us and heal us in the midst of it!

The very next verse, Hebrews 4:16, helps us understand this quandary of how we can allow Christ to heal: "Let us then with confidence draw near to the throne of grace, that we may receive mercy and find grace to help in time of need." Due to His understanding, we can confidently draw near to the throne of God for healing and mercy and grace! Again, there was such a difference in my life of knowing these truths in my head and *knowing* them in my heart. The translation from the head to the heart is a difficult one at times. My heart was wounded. I felt alone, exposed, rejected, angry, bitter, and betrayed. Hearing that there is understanding and healing was one thing, but actually experiencing it was a completely new and different thing.

---

13   Frank Viola, *God's Favorite Place on Earth* (Colorado Springs: David C. Cook, 2013), 28.

JESUS ALONE SUFFERED AS WE HAVE

When one surveys the vast plethora of religions, theories, or scientific thought out there, not a single one promises to understand your pain, much less bring healing—*except* Jesus. Inner peace is not healing; it's the purposeful ignoring of real pain and the shutting down of true emotions. So, many would ask: "What good is Jesus?" To them I always share this truth: that Jesus understands our pain and can heal us from it. No amount of research can bring one to a healing place. No amount of "emptying oneself" can actually bring about the end of our sorrows. Nothing can truly free us from our wounds other than an understanding and healing God, both of which we find in Jesus Himself. Even among many followers of Christ, there is still a loss of healing, even if we can admit He understands. Why is this and how could this possibly be the case? David, the King and Psalmist, was one familiar with sorrows, pain, and many wounds, yet he was also one who experienced the goodness and the healing of God. David beautifully gives reason why so many miss it when he said: *"Oh, taste and see that the Lord is good! Blessed is the man who takes refuge in him!"* (Psalm 34:8).

I fear the reason why many miss the realities of Jesus' healing (which stems from His understanding) is because so few have tasted Him. Many churchgoing religionists will know *about* Jesus, sing *about* Him, and even like what they know *about* Him, but few people actually taste Him and eat of His goodness. Many Christians are content with head knowledge and completely miss the *heart* knowledge aspect of the faith. Few people taste God and experience His fullness and are completely content with this lack! Friend, I hope you are not one of them, but if you are, let me challenge you to taste His goodness. He has healing for the pain He so deeply understands, and He desires you to receive the healing He's offering!

When you approach God in prayer, what is your goal? Is your goal to dump all of the day's issues upon Him, ask for help, and then walk away? Is your goal to go through a set list of prayers (which are now memorized) so you can mark it off of a list? Is your goal to know God and reveal more of yourself to Him in the process through listening and honest conversation?

Whichever of these you picked may be an indication of why you may have not been experiencing the full freedom from your pain that God has for you. As a religionist, it is easy to go with a list, pray it, and be done. As a wanderer, it is easy to dump issues and ask for help, but as a person seeking to actually *know* the one to whom you're speaking, those avenues are difficult and almost impossible. Jesus desires to heal us and for us to taste His goodness, but if we don't sit to *hear* His voice whisper truth and healing into us, we will miss it completely. Because we've missed His truth, we will blame Him for not taking away our pains, or even decry His ability to understand them. We will believe the lie that we are unimportant to Him and begin a process of bitter pursuit of something else that will satisfy, yet nothing else will ever satisfy.

Many religionists will find deeper solace in the more "religious" activities they can consume their lives with. The wanderer will wander to many lovers' beds seeking the intimacy of *knowing* and *being known* that their souls are begging for, yet will continue to come up empty time and time again. Both avenues of seeker (the religionist and the wanderer) will be worse off than when they left and will have a trail of lovers or wounded people in their wake, but will still not find healing from their pain.

Jesus does understand our pain and He does bring healing, we simply need to truly *know* Him and ask for it. When He left, He told His disciples to wait because He was going to send them (and us) the Helper, who would make everything make sense and would bring about the true intimacy they were losing with Him leaving. With the Helper, they'd understand the Scriptures; they'd receive power to heal (and be healed). They'd *know* the heart of God; they'd *taste* the riches of the divine relationship, and they would go forth and share the great message with others. We can't just know about God, we must know Him and in so doing we will see the understanding He has for our pains as well as *know* the healing.

Recently, I've been preaching through the book of Revelation, and John also bumped into this truth of truly *knowing* God in the book of Revelation. In Revelation 10, we see this large, intimidating angel coming from Heaven, and he has a tiny scroll in his hand. A voice from heaven tells John to go, take and eat the scroll; it will be sweet as honey in your mouth, but bitter to your stomach. John walks over to this angel and, probably out of fear, asks the angel to just hand him the scroll. The angel denies the request and tells John to take the scroll and then to eat it.

What does this have to do with *knowing* God? In his book *Reversed Thunder*, Eugene Peterson says, "Eating a book takes it all in, assimilating it into the tissue of your life."[14] This idea of eating God's Word resonated with me and immediately brought me back to this whole conversation that knowing God can help heal our pain. I think too often we are content to know *about* God, but we don't *taste* His goodness, like was discussed above. I see this imagery as I would approach my favorite food: buffalo chicken pizza. I can know everything there is to know about this food; how it's made, what ingredients go into it, and even how to make it. Yet, it is food, and to truly *know* it, I would need to allow my whole body to experience it, not just my brain. My mouth, my stomach, my eyes, and my nose are all involved in eating something. You can't know food unless you eat it. God is the same way! We must allow our whole selves to experience Him; our hunger for God can truly only be satisfied if we taste Him and eat His Word.

Now, before we get all religionist about what this looks like and start building extra-biblical rules to this, what am I really saying? I'm not saying there are a set number of hours we need to be in the Word in order to eat it and taste Him. I'm not saying the answer to all your problems is "just read the Bible more." I'm not even laying on a heavy-handed guilt that demands you be reading your Bible more than you have. I am saying that if we are to truly *know* God, it is important to chew on His Word and eat it. It's not the checklist Christianity

---

14   H. Eugene Peterson, *Reversed Thunder: The Revelation of John and the Praying Imagination* (New York: HarperOne, 1988), 107.

the religionist holds to, nor is it the whimsical reading of whatever Scripture happens to pop up when I open my Bible. I'm talking about asking God to speak to your heart by the power of the Spirit within you. I'm talking about sitting and wrestling with a Scripture that bugs you internally, not ignoring the fact that it bothers you, but actually taking time to wrestle through it. I'm talking about a conversation with God, not reading of the Bible as if it is a good novel.

KNOWING GOD EXPOSES HIS UNDERSTANDING

God desires for us to know Him, and when we *know* Him, we can see how He understands our pain and can bring healing to us. Jesus is good, trustworthy, and has the power to heal our pains and wounds. No other religion deals with pain this way. Many say to simply become one with your pain and use it to your advantage. Others say to simply suck it up and deal with your suffering on your own. Still others say to completely forget your problems and don't allow them to hinder your chi; bad things happen, so forget it and move on! Jesus acknowledges your pain, even helps expose the hidden pains, then *heals* them so they are no longer a hindrance to us truly living the life He desires for us to live. So go ahead and give Him your pain; let Him set you *free*!

When wondering through this idea of suffering and pain, Christ's healing, and the issues that pop up within the church in dealing with these things, I became frustrated. I was frustrated because I began to realize that one of the things that often gets neglected in church is the space and need to grieve. Often when something traumatic happens, we allow people a period of time for grief, but then try to urge them to "lean on God" and get over it. Sometimes it takes longer to grieve than many of us give room for, and soon we begin to judge people's faith based on how long they end up grieving. Other people have hidden wounds they feel are "too small" to grieve and are afraid of being judged if they share it as a grievance. In short, for many, the church is not a place to receive comfort from their pain, and I feel this is a weakness we must correct. Revelation says, "God will wipe away every tear from their eyes" (Rev. 7:17b).

I believe from this passage that when we get in front of the throne, we will be able to share our grievances from earth with God. It will be a healing process with our Abba Father and He will hear our pain and wipe away every tear from our eyes. In effect, we will be comforted. Those sealed (Rev. 7:3 and Eph. 1:13-14) will be comforted and every tear we shed in our grief will be wiped away. We will receive healing from God. All the pain will be gone, all the wounds healed, and all the issues wiped off the slate.

God knows of the deep need for us to be comforted. He knows the deep-seated reality that we can't move forward until our past has been healed. We may think we can move on by ourselves, we may pretend we can, but we can't. That's why before we enter into Glory He will wipe away every tear from our eyes!

One of the great realities about the book of Revelation is that we see Heaven is a now and not yet reality. This comfort, this tear wiping can be ours now. We might not be able to receive the fullness that we will once in Heaven, but we can have a portion now. As the church, we could be the place of healing for the past wounds people have. We could be praying for healing over the lives of every person in church. We could be praying Heaven down into the lives of one another, yet this portion of God's promises seems to have been forgotten.

Instead in large part, many people I've talked to are afraid to share what ails their soul, and at church most of all! Jesus once said: "Blessed are those who mourn, for they shall be comforted" (Matt. 5:4), which not only gives us permission to mourn our grief but also promises that if we do so, it won't be empty when we do—we will receive comfort from Him!

As the expression of God on this earth, we could be a healing balm to this world by lending comfort to the mourning. Have we abdicated this to counselors or psychologists? In large part, I believe we have! Let us become a safe place for the mourners and seek to bring them comfort through the power of the Spirit and allow God to wipe our tears as well!

WHAT GOOD IS JESUS THEN?

How could God allow suffering and pain in the world? If He really were good, wouldn't these be easily eliminated? Suffering is the human condition. Without it, we wouldn't know joy. Joy comes because we understand suffering as well. Jesus suffered alongside of us. He became human in part to understand our suffering and to show us by His life that He could relate. Many people say it was an act of godly child abuse to let Him suffer and die the way He did, but it was actually a willing act to show through a life that He could relate to His creation. Jesus is good because instead of eliminating suffering, He experienced it. He is good because He then made way for healing through His Spirit. We can't cover up or ignore our suffering, because we will just end up finding a coping mechanism. We need to feel it, grieve it, and allow the only God to ever experience and understand it to then heal us from it.

REFLECTIONS ON "JESUS UNDERSTANDS OUR SUFFERING"

1. Have you ever looked at your suffering and said: "NO ONE understands!?"

2. What are your thoughts/reactions to Jesus understanding your pain? Do you agree?

3. Why is it so important to have deep, knowing intimacy with God?

JESUS OFFERS FORGIVENESS

IN A WORLD OBSESSED WITH performance, failure can be devastating. Shame settles in when one feels as if he or she just doesn't measure up, or a solemn admittance that one can never measure up, so they accept their fate and stop attempting anything worthwhile. Both sides are catastrophic and detrimental to people, yet it goes un-discussed and the whole issue itself is undervalued. If you perform well, you are well-liked, even loved or adored. If you mess up, there is very little grace and even less forgiveness. Many people wander through life knowing they don't have it all together. The human condition is to know we are not perfect, but is there a way to be forgiven my mistakes no matter how big or how small? There are many people in this world who mess up, and a good number (not all however) of those people are trying to seek forgiveness or healing from the mistakes they've made in life. Does Jesus offer such a forgiveness that can both heal and take the weight of compounded guilt away? I personally believe He does.

PERFORMANCE-BASED LIVING

Systems based on performance can be people killers because each person is trying to keep up with the performance machine, and if many are keeping pace and performing well, others see that as a threat and try to "out-perform" the "competition." Instead of a team collaborative effect, you get a group seeking personal glory and effectively killing people in the process. Every culture struggles with this issue of performance. People of certain cultures, like my Asian friends, have it slightly worse than other ethnic groups as it pertains to performance in every aspect of life, but the pressure to perform is still prevalent in every culture. This constant drive to perform, no matter what the cost, leaks into our expectations of God or whatever expression of a "higher being" we may think of.

PERFORMANCE-BASED RELIGION

When you take this whole issue of performance-driven living down to the level of religion, we can see the deeper, more psychological effects that take place in such a toxic ideology. The thought quickly comes to the surface that: "If I perform well for my God, He will be happy with me. If I screw up, He will be angry and will take His anger out upon me, my family, my job, or anything I hold dear." For many religions, such as the Muslim faith, this is how they proclaim their god to be: angry and ready to pounce on the poor little screw-ups of the earth. Many in the church live this way as well; thinking that Jesus is the same and the Father who sent Him is the same—that His desire is to bring wrath upon the non-performers of the earth. The perception they received from their experience with Christianity was that their performance and how they behaved was ultimately the largest concern God had for their lives. This in turn creates a culture of performance-driven righteousness. It becomes the driving force behind secret sins and keeping certain struggles in the shadows. This perception can also be largely dictated by the kind of father one grew up with, not solely church experience, but this performance-based view of Christianity still occurs from church experiences more often then I would care to admit. Looking at Christianity in this light then brings people to a place where they look upon the church and Jesus, of whom they are to be image bearers, and say that "No, this will not bring forgiveness, only more guilt."

I recently chatted with a young adult who shared that her family's car trips to church consisted of a detailed list of what you could say and not say in church. Instead of the normal run down of bad and good words, his parents listed all the things they as parents were doing wrong as topics not to be discussed and the good things they were doing as parents as good fodder for discussion. The father, an elder in the church, made sure his children gave a book and chapter of the

Bible they were supposedly going through as a family for devotions, but he wasn't actually taking the time to have that Bible study time with his family. He told his family that the elders all made a vow to do family devotions, so if anyone asked, the family was definitely to say their father was doing family devotions. The father told his children in essence: "I'm to perform at a certain level and since I'm not performing, I need you to lie and say I am so I can still look good."

This story is true, and there are many more out there just like it where people inside the church believe the lie that everyone cares about performance, even God. By that logic, we need to be on our best behavior, and if by chance we're not on our best behavior, we need to fake it to the other church people so they think we are close with God. This quickly becomes a toxic environment where being honest is shunned and lies prevail. Satan is the author of lies, so he is more than ready for this type of environment to become the norm in churches today—and sadly he's been winning over a lot of churches with this one.

We quickly forget that God is a God of forgiveness and a God of second, third, fourth, fifth, etc. chances! I recently wrote a devotional for the men in our congregation based off of the father in the story of the Prodigal Son. I want to share what I wrote here because I believe it cuts right to the heart of what I'm trying to convey.

A FATHER WHO RUNS TO US

And he arose and came to his father. But while he was still a long way off, his father saw him and felt compassion, and ran and embraced him and kissed him. And the son said to him, "Father, I have sinned against heaven and before you. I am no longer worthy to be called your son." But the father said to his servants, "Bring quickly the best robe, and put it on him, and put a ring on his hand, and shoes on his feet. And bring the fattened calf and kill it, and let us eat and celebrate. For this my son was dead, and is alive again; he was lost, and is found.' And they began to celebrate (Luke 15:20-24).

Most Jewish men in the culture in which this story is set would have disowned their son and threw him back out on the street. Most Jewish men would have shamed their son and cut him out of their family, and this would have been done in order to save face in front of the community. In essence the father would be covering his own backside, caring more for his reputation than for his son. Yet, this father was different. He waited and even yearned for the return of his son. He planned his son's restoration before his son even realized he needed restored. God has done the very same thing for us. If God cared more about His own reputation, He'd have disowned all of us, and not a single one of us would be fit to enter into His Kingdom. Yet He ran to us and was planning our restoration way before we knew we needed it.

As parents, we must live this way. We have huge sway over the formation of our children's identity. The way we behave and speak into their lives helps them understand who they are and who God is. When our kids miss the mark, no matter how big or how small, shame should not be our response. As fathers and mothers, we should model God's example and run to our children in their brokenness, embrace them, kiss them, and love on them. No matter how young or old, no matter how silly or severe the mistakes they made were, we should model God and run to them.

I may not always think this aloud, or admit to thinking this, but I sometimes think: "People will judge me on my child's behavior, so I need to be severe in my punishments so they shape up and make me look good." I must remember that my child is more important than my image. I must cultivate my children's hearts, not to try and change their behavior, the same way God cultivates my heart. He points out my behavior and shows me in His Word, which actions are right and wrong. However, He also knows that bad behavior is ultimately a heart issue, and if He runs to me and captures my heart, my behavior will automatically change because His love has transformed me. I will no longer desire to rebel in bad behavior. Let us then be men who run to our children and cultivate their hearts!

As parents, we can take this reality to heart! I recently began praying a prayer to help keep this story fresh in my mind and heart: "Lord, I pray that You will stop me when I am about to shame my child. Holy Spirit, silence my mouth if I am to speak or do anything contrary to what You would do. Help me to be a man who runs to my children and be a daddy like You who cultivates their hearts! Amen."

COMING CLOSE TO THE HEART OF GOD

I stated I think this gets to the heart of the matter, because simply put: *Jesus forgives*. When we can truly see Him as the Daddy running to us, we can then in turn run to our children because *it's not about their behavior, it's about their hearts*. When we see God as a mean guy trying to change our behaviors, it seems He cares only about the outside appearance and how we are making Him look. Yet, He seeks to grab our hearts because He knows once He has our hearts, our behaviors will be changed, not because He's making us change but because His love and His heart will have changed us so completely that we won't want to do those things anymore.

To elaborate on this, I heard an amazing story of two hearts. Some doctors decided to do an experiment with two different hearts. These hearts were beating at their own pace and rhythm. They then took the two hearts and connected them to where they were touching. Immediately the hearts began to beat as one, no more separate paces or rhythms, just one pace and one rhythm. When we get so close to our Father and our hearts touch, our heart begins to beat as one with His and the sinful and dangerous things in which we used to seek refuge no longer appeal to us. We have all that we need within this deep, rich and intimate relationship with the Father.

Many of us reading this book will most likely know John 3:16: "For God so loved the world, that he gave his only Son, that whoever believes in him should not perish but have eternal life." However, sometimes we forget the very next verse: "For God did not send his Son into the world to condemn the world, but in order that the world might be saved through him (17)." Here, we see God's heart for the world in which He sent His only Son—He desires the world to be saved through Jesus. He does not want to condemn anyone, He desires all of us to be saved. Now, let me state not everyone *is* saved as pastors like Rob Bell seem to allude to in their books, but God's heart is *for* global salvation.

WE ALL NEED FORGIVENESS

The world is broken and in need of being rescued. Although the world may not openly admit these words, it does agree with this premise. The world would have to agree because one can't turn the TV on without seeing some devastating news of catastrophe brought about by human decisions. Many of the popular films people are drawn to revolve around the world in peril and heroes coming in and rescuing them. The narrative theme of "needing a hero" is extremely in vogue and has been for a long time. Deep within the human soul is a knowing desire for the need to be rescued and forgiven. This desire is why Jesus came—to save the world—but not just by swooping in and beating up the bad guys as is the popular idea of a Savior; rather, Jesus came as a missionary. Jesus was the first missionary, sent on a mission from God to be God in the flesh, to dwell among us, and to be with us and lovingly direct us to Himself, where we would find healing, restoration, redemption, forgiveness, and life.

Many people seek to find their salvation in other things like money, sex, fame, and status; yet Jesus was clear—salvation is *through Him* and nothing else. Love drove Him to be our Savior. Love drove Him from Heaven to the crib and from the crib to the cross. Jesus came on a rescue mission to save the world. This is big news—*good news!*—news we all need to be reminded of.

Yet Jesus' mission of bringing salvation only began with His birth and continued on after His death! After His ascension, He then sent His Spirit to indwell *us* (those who believe), so we can continue His mission of dwelling among the world to continue His mission to lovingly direct us towards Himself, the only place we would find healing, restoration, redemption, forgiveness, and life! He is the example of how to live out the gospel, why to do it, and what it looks like to do it. If Jesus brings forgiveness, shouldn't we too be people of forgiveness? This is where *living* out the gospel is tough. There will be times we will find the need to deny ourselves and love others through the avenue of forgiveness when all we want to do is make others suffer as we have. We don't desire to be people who run to those who hurt us, but in order to be like Jesus, we need to show the reality that Jesus does in fact forgive. As image bearers of Christ, we have not displayed the running to and forgiving aspect of Christ enough! How many non-Christians do we "do life" with on a regular basis? If the answer is few to none, maybe God is challenging you and me to purposefully seek out ways in which we can be Jesus to the dark places of this world, to take up His mantle of the Mission to save the world *through Jesus* instead of being on the sidelines simply condemning the world.

Why share this? I think it proves God is a God that runs to His children. He desires to get our hearts; He desires for our lives to be saved by His touch through Jesus administered by the Holy Spirit. He is a forgiving God and sent His Son to prove this point. Are there certain restrictions or lists of things that God states we should and shouldn't do? Yes, there are. Yet these restrictions exist to show us how we as humans will best function, *and* they show us we can't do it without His forgiving touch. We need the blood of the Lamb and the indwelling Spirit in order to live the life He calls those of us who are saved to live.

WHAT GOOD IS JESUS? AND WHAT PURPOSE DOES HE SERVE?

In our world that is full of relativism, activism, socialism, atheism, and a whole bunch of other "isms," what good is Jesus? He brings forgiveness. Nothing else in this world can bring this sense of forgiveness like Jesus can. His purpose was to die in order to make forgiveness possible. It's part of His mission statement. It's the reason for so much of what He did in His life; and we all *need* and *crave* forgiveness, whether or not we think we do, we all do. We've all failed. We've all messed up. No one living or who has lived (save for one person) has lived a perfect life. When you look back at the story of your life, where do you feel the most regret? Who are the people that you've wounded? Where do you feel inadequate due to the things in which you've done wrong? There's forgiveness for that.

When you look back on the story of your life, what are the words and actions you committed that you know were wrong? Who have you lost that you didn't get to apologize to? There's forgiveness for that.

Slowly we see that everyone has a need for forgiveness. Many of us may not have thought of these things in light of a Holy God, but we've sinned against Him and due to that, we all deserve death. Yet, even for such a crime, there is forgiveness for that. God desires for us to know and share the story of forgiveness, not just to know it cognitively, but also to experience and feel it.

I fear that many of us who have walked with Jesus for a long period of our lives have forgotten the experience of forgiveness and have opted to sense it cognitively rather than experientially. I say this because I know it to be true for myself. I ask God to "forgive me of my sins," but it becomes an intellectual exercise. I know in my head God forgives, but I still walk around with the guilt and shame of what I've done. I've not been freed from this burden that forgiveness lifts off of me. I walk around pretending to fully understand the full forgiveness of God but haven't truly known it for some time.

You'll know it when it comes. It's like a weighted blanket being lifted off of you. You become lighter, more free, and more joyful than before. You sense a new feeling of relief and excitement all bundled into one. It's a powerful sense of elation and too often we neglect to allow the Spirit of God to free us experientially from our sins. People easily return to old habits and ask the same prayer of forgiveness over and over again. Mind you, God will continue to forgive, but He wants us to actually *feel* it!

Let me encourage you, whether you're a newbie at this or an old timer, to sit and ask God to forgive you of your sins. Stay in a posture of humility and admittance and ask the Spirit of God to allow you to sense His forgiveness. Ask the Lord to take the burden of this junk off of your heart. The cross has made it possible to be forgiven, so it's there for us to grab a hold of. Don't be content with just *knowing* you are forgiven; ask God for a sense of *peace* that comes with the forgiveness.Jesus is good because He forgives!

REFLECTIONS ON "JESUS OFFERS FORGIVENESS"

1. "No one else can forgive me like Jesus can." Do you agree with this? Why or why not?

2. When you ask for forgiveness of your sins and "junk" in your life, do you wait to *experience* it, or not?

3. Why would Jesus bringing forgiveness be such an important message to this world?

JESUS IS THE SAVIOR

SUPERMAN, THE MAN OF STEEL, is an amazing character in the comic world. He stands for truth, justice, and the American way, but he stands for so much more than that. Very few people actually know that Superman comes from two Jewish men who had a Messianic longing. These two men specifically designed Superman to be the image of the Messiah they longed for, one who was strong, invincible, and on the side of the downtrodden, for peace, for justice and for truth.[15]

As you read this, I am sure you are shaking your head in disbelief, but I assure you it is true. Look at Superman's (Kal-El's) story for one second. He was sent forth as the hope of Krypton because Krypton was about to be destroyed. He was sent on a ship to the only hope of a place that could keep him (as well as strengthen him). He was found, adopted, and raised to know he was special, yet his true identity was hidden for a time.

Looking at this story, it is eerily similar to that of Moses, the first "messiah," if you will, of the Jewish people! Superman was designed to depict the longing in the heart of the Jewish people, the picture of the Messiah they so desperately desired as well as what they hoped he would be. Kal-El, Superman's Kryptonian name, in Hebrew means: "Equal to or greater than God."

As this idea hits you a little bit I hope you're asking why would any of this be relevant to anything pertaining to Jesus? Superman as a figure is highly popular. Many people like Superman because of the idea of who he is. He's a Savior, one who brings freedom, safety, justice,

---

15   "Mensch of Steel: Superman's Jewish Roots," Den of Geek, accessed November 1, 2015, http://www.denofgeek.us/books-comics/superman/231283/mensch-of-steel-supermans-jewish-roots.

mercy, grace, and salvation from many different things. It is truly my belief that the human soul has a love for heroes (as I stated in the previous chapter), not because we are natural geeks who love comics, but because within us is a cry for a hero. The creators of Superman felt it and so do those who religiously (no pun intended) follow every move Superman makes.

A great illustration of our desperation comes in the movie *Superman Returns*. The scene opens where Superman is taking Lois up for a "romantic flight" when he says, "What do you hear?"

To which Lois replies, "Nothing."

Superman continues, "Well, I hear everything. You once wrote that the world doesn't need a Savior, but everyday I hear people crying out or one."

I could ask the same question to everyone in the world. I could ask them for a moment to consider the reality of God if they don't already: "What do you think God hears?" My response would be simply: "I know God hears people crying out for a Savior." That scene in *Superman Returns* depicts that perfectly. The world in general doesn't think they need a Savior, but if they were to listen to the cries of their own hearts and the world's, they'd hear desperate cries for salvation. As I alluded to earlier, I think this deep-seated desire for salvation shows itself in our fandom of heroes. We see amazing people bringing huge amounts of freedom and safety from evil and something within us screams: "YES! We *need* that!"

WHY THE WORLD NEEDS A SAVIOR

Paul's language on the strong, binding grip of our sinful nature is very clear in Romans. He says things like: "For while we were living in the flesh, our sinful passions, aroused by the law, were at work in our members, to bear fruit for death" (Rom. 7:5). Also Romans 6:23a says, "For the wages of sin is death." The sinful nature doesn't only bind us here on earth to be sinners, but it effects our eternal lives as well. The death Paul is talking about is not only a physical death, but also an eternal death. That is what God meant in the Garden of Eden when He told Adam and Eve that the fruit from the tree of good and evil would cause death. He didn't just mean death of the body, but death of the eternal soul as well, meaning that man's final destiny without the Savior would be damnation in hell for all eternity! Being bound to our sinful natures will ultimately cause the damnation of our eternal souls. Sin is the nature of men. Romans 3:23 states, "For all have sinned and fall short of the glory of God." And in Romans 3:10 the Word says, "As it is written: 'None is righteous, no, not one.'" By our human nature, we do nothing but fall into sin; it is our inherent nature to disobey God. When you see two-year-old children refusing to listen to their parents, we see how natural it is for us to refuse to listen to our Heavenly Father. Without Christ, we are bound to the sinful nature and can in fact do nothing outside of sin; we are prisoners of sin and are in desperate need of salvation. However, Romans 6:23b also holds a promise, "But the free gift of God is eternal life in Christ Jesus our Lord," thus defining and outlining Christ as our conduit of salvation! Christ is our Savior; His death freed us from the bondage and slavery we had to the sinful nature. We must receive and accept this gift; it isn't forced upon us, and we must accept it.

HOW CAN JESUS BE THE ONE?

How can one be confident that this reality of Jesus is true and that He is the "Savior?" How can we claim this truth or assist those who don't believe in seeing it to be true? When one looks at other religions and their idea of "salvation," or their answer to the brokenness of man, the answer is always found in the adherence to the religion, not necessarily in the deity. What this means is that the onus of one's salvation is on the person's ability to follow the laws and demands of the deity. The laws and demands are the "gift" and the "way" to salvation, but it is the duty of the religion-follower to make his or her own efforts to get to the promised salvation. Jesus is the only God who died and made a way.

When it comes to the plan and purpose of atonement (cleansing), we first have to look at two ideas: the nature of God and the nature of the Law. These two ideas form the reason and purpose for the necessity of atonement. The nature of God is pure perfection; there is no blemish, no scar, and nothing to cause imperfection. This being known, the idea, thought, and act of sin is completely and utterly disgusting to God. He can't stand to be near sin because it is 100% contrary to His being.

When it comes to the nature of the Law, I believe that Millard Erickson describes it well when he says: "The Law should be seen as the expression of God's person and will. He does not command love and forbid murder simply because he decides to do so." Erickson also says that "the law is something of a transcript of the nature of God."[16] Erickson, I think, gets right to the true nature of the Law when he says, "Disobeying it (the Law) is actually an attack upon the very nature of God Himself. . . . The law is understood as a means of relating to a personal God."[17] The nature of the Law is to be God's guideline for us to live a life to the full extent just as He intended it to be. If we were to live a "lawful" life fulfilling the whole law, our lives would be lived the way that God intended it to be—perfect. However, we are sinful beings and could *never* fulfill the whole Law for our whole lives.

This, I believe, is the second purpose for the Law: to show us our own absolute *need* for God. The Laws of Moses that were given by God Himself were to point out the very fact that no human could follow them 100% of the time. They were meant to be an arrow pointing to our *need* of God. Instead, many took them as a way of earning their salvation, as is the case with every other religion. Much of the certainty of Christ's title of "Savior" comes from the reality that no other religion uses their law as an arrow pointing to our inadequacy and then makes a way for us despite our inability to adhere to the law.

Paul alludes to the idea constantly when he discusses the Law in Galatians. Who among us men could fulfill the law our whole lives to

---

16   Millard J. Erickson, *Introducing Christian Doctrine* (Grand Rapids: Baker Academic, 2001), 257.

17   Ibid.

perfection? The answer is no one: "No one does good, not even one" (Rom. 3:12; Psalm 14:1-3; 53:1-3; Eccles. 7:20). This is why I have full confidence when I say the second purpose for the Law was to show us our need for Christ. If the Law wasn't there, we wouldn't know how depraved we really are. Nor would we be able to see that there is an all-Holy God waiting to help us in our depravity. Through the Law, we see God's love, judgment, and love again. We see His love in creating such a law so we can live life to the fullest, His judgment when we fail to follow the Law, and His love again when He gives us an atoning sacrifice to appease the punishment.

When it comes to the Law, I always feel it best to liken it to a design. God is the great designer, and He knows how His design works best, so He lays out the things that are to be done for optimum efficiency as well as the things not to be done. This then shows the true intent of God; it's not a tool of control but rather instructions on how we are wired and designed to be the best, most efficient, us.

The lack of following these instructions then brings us to the fact that we need to find a way to atone for these transgressions. If no one is good, how do we receive God's blessings? How do we become clean before God, and how does our sin become eradicated before an all-Holy God? The answer of atonement lies in the sacrifice of Christ on the cross.

SACRIFICE IS REQUIRED FOR ATONEMENT

This sacrifice of Jesus, taking on our sin and dying in our place, brought about the atonement of our sins. There is a price to pay for sin and the price was and will always be death. In the Old Testament, this death was signified in the sacrifice of the prized lamb. Numbers 28:3-8 describes such an atoning sacrifice that was required. The sins of the people required the blood of the lamb to wash away their sins, thus causing atonement for the people. The plan for Christ's life was always for Him to be our atoning sacrifice, the Lamb whose blood was shed on our behalf to atone for our sins. However, His death and blood not only covered us for a year alone (as the Old Testament sacrifice did), but for eternity, and another sacrifice would never be required again. His blood was and is enough to atone every sin from the beginning to the end; His blood has brought about the cleansing of all who accept Him and claim Him as Lord and Savior!

The lamb that was required for sacrifice in the Old Testament was to be a perfect lamb. It could have no blemishes, no faults, simply a perfect lamb so that the untainted lamb could offer its blood to wash the sins of the people white as snow. Christ was such a lamb; this is why He is the *real* Superman! His life was lived by the Spirit with perfection. There was no sin, no blemish in Him. He was the God-Man who walked the earth without sin, and thus His sacrifice was the perfect covering for our sins. When Christ hung on the cross, He not only became cursed for us ("a hanged man is cursed by God" Deut. 21:23b), but also took on every sin ever committed or that would be committed. When Christ hung on the tree, God had to avert His eyes from His Son, which was the reason why Christ shouted, "My God, My God, why have you forsaken me"? (Matt. 27:46b). The purpose of this sacrifice was this very thing: to bring about the cleansing of all sin from that moment until eternity, so all may have the chance to accept Christ and live forever with Him in heaven!

When discussing Christ as the real Superman, the real Savior, one must discuss the idea(s) represented by justification. An excellent definition of justification comes from Erickson in his book *Introducing Christian Doctrine*: "Justification is God's action pronouncing sinners righteous in His sight."[18] It is in this idea of justification that we can find ourselves clean and blameless before the almighty, all-Holy God. When we are declared justified, the stains of our sin no longer appear on us; we are 100% clean, 100% right before God. Being righteous in God's sight is being set back to the way we always should've been before the fall of man in Genesis 3. When Adam and Eve sinned, they caused the

---

18   Millard J. Erickson, *Introducing Christian Doctrine* (Grand Rapids: Baker Academic, 2001), 317.

rest of mankind to be cursed with the sinful nature. However, Christ, who was the second Adam, or rather as Adam should've been (perfect and blameless), came to the earth and lived the life we should've. He then eliminated the curse of sin with His death on the cross! When we accept this truth and ask the Lord to be Lord of our lives we are accepting the gift of Christ's death and embracing the justification that it brings.

Through the blood of Jesus, we are washed clean and proclaimed blameless before the throne of God. We are not only blameless, but by the very definition of justification, when we accept the death of Christ and believe in Him, we are declared as having fulfilled all the requirements of the Law. We are wholly cleansed and wholly accepted into Heaven, making perfect that which was not perfect. This is the true power of justification, the fact that we are cleansed of our sins as well as being made perfect in the fulfillment of the law.

So, we return to our original question from the beginning of this book: What good is Jesus? This perfection is *only* possible by the sacrifice of the cross of Jesus Christ! That is why Jesus says: "I am the way, and the truth and the life. No one comes to the Father except through me" (John 14:6). Jesus made the way possible, knowing we could not do it on our own. We, on our own, are more wretched and wicked than any other living thing; it is only through Jesus, His death and His resurrection, that we can be proclaimed blameless. Without the justification that His death brings, we would be considered filthy rags before our Father and there would be no hope for eternal life, only the expectation of eternal condemnation. This is the truth and crux of the Christian faith, that Christ's death and resurrection causes us to become blameless in the sight of God, because had Christ not died nor resurrected from the grave, death wouldn't have been defeated, nor would the curse of sin. In *Introducing Christian Doctrine*, Erickson sums it up well when he says: "The act of justification is not a matter of God's announcing that sinners are something they are not. There is a constitutive aspect to justification as well. For what God does is actually to constitute us righteous by imputing (not imparting) the righteousness of Christ to us."[19]

Meaning that God doesn't just say, "Hey you're righteous now," but He imputes us with this righteousness. I always get an image of a Boston Cream donut when I think of this imputing righteousness, because Christ's death takes out the gunk in our shell. He sucks out all the sin and dirt in us. Then when we are empty, He fills us anew with the righteousness of Christ. Similar to an empty-shelled donut being filled with cream, that is the *imputation* of the righteousness of Christ. Praise God that He doesn't just say "Okay, you're righteous," but sucks the bad out and gives us a new life. That is the truth of justification and regeneration!

ENCOUNTERING CHRIST AS SAVIOR

My first encounter of Christ as Savior happened when I was three years old. My dad was preaching about Heaven and Hell, and I was frightened to death of burning in Hell for all eternity. So when we got home, I asked my dad how I could receive this Jesus as my personal Lord and Savior and, at the tender age of three, said the "sinner's prayer." I realized then that He was my Savior, my rescuer, and my lifeguard in the swimming pool of Hell and eternal death, but the full realization didn't hit until about eleven. My parents got divorced when I was only eight years old. My family was going through a really rough time, and I discovered the art of rebellion. At eight years old, I was drinking alcohol, smoking cigarettes, and trying to be as bad a kid as I could be. I lived with my mom, so my dad's ever-watchful gaze wasn't there, thus I engaged in such behavior. My sister was also enjoying her newfound freedom, but my brother, however, remained a faithful young man. He insisted on going to youth group and doing the church thing, while my sister and I decided to stray away from that.

Seeing my brother's desire for God sort of caused a questioning inside of myself. I saw my sister leaving the idea of Christ as Savior and

---

my brother clinging to it. My brother seemed happier, more excited about life, and all around just plain better. *I was having fun, but I saw something in my brother that I wanted.* One day when I was about nine, I was smoking in the house, and my brother threatened to call our mom to tell her that I was smoking. I didn't believe him, so I continued puffing at my cigarette; however, he called our mom. My mom didn't yell and flip out, but what struck me was my brother didn't like who I had become.

I soon stopped smoking and started to get involved with Bible Quizzing at my church. I threw my whole self into it and came out deeply affected by God. We were going through the book of Matthew that year and seeing the life of Christ made me want my relationship with Him. I re-dedicated my life to Christ at the age of ten and have been following hard after Him ever since.

The toils in my life, the struggles of a kid and adolescent in the midst of divorce, were terrible! I didn't want anything to do with this Christ I learned about at an early age. It seemed He didn't care about the troubles in my life, so why did I want Him? However, Christ the Savior took ahold of me and wouldn't let me go. I have seen Him bring back my father from the brink of death, my sister from sure disease, my mom from spiritual death, my brother through depression and doubt, myself through my parents' divorce, and watching a suicide attempt, rebellion, and depression.

I have seen Christ as Savior throughout my life and I have seen Him save many who needed His salvation. He is the real Superman this world is longing for.

What good is Jesus? He's a real, true, authentic hero. Jesus is good because He is a Savior.

REFLECTIONS ON "JESUS IS THE SAVIOR"

1. Did you know about the Jewish origins of Superman, that he was the depiction of a messianic longing?

2. How can Jesus be your Savior in this moment, right now?

    .

3. What is the hardest portion to accept of Jesus being a Savior?

JESUS MAKES US BETTER

NO MATTER WHO YOU ARE, I think we can agree to the fact that we are not perfect. In fact, the closer you are to my generation the more this idea is openly admitted. We have flaws and are people who know they mess up and our lives are far from being clean; we waste too much time trying to cover up our mistakes, so let's just be up front and admit our failures.

So if we can say we're not perfect and have flaws, then we must ask, is there a way to become better people? How can we live life and continue to improve ourselves? Isn't this some of pop culture's allure? It offers some "solutions" to our problems and sells us a product to add to our lives for the betterment of ourselves. These products get bought, used, and thrown out because many of them held empty promises or were too difficult to actually implement. Our desire to become better shows how our souls long for something more. The human heart knows deep down that there is more, something that can truly transform us, make us whole, and make us better. Jesus is the real, true solution to this longing. Jesus is good because He makes us better.

I understand that this is going to be a bit hard to swallow, and some of you disagree with the main premise, but go with me, because I've seen it played out in my life so many times. Jesus died for our salvation; He is the real Superman as we established in the previous chapter. He rose from the grave and He conquered death. These are the "biggies" of the Jesus story, yet many of us miss the power of His life.

THE POWER OF JESUS' LIFE

Jesus, while on earth, was fully God and fully man. Here He lived out a dependent relationship with the Holy Spirit. Jesus succumbed to the limitations of humanity in order to show us how to live a life of Holiness—surrendered to the Spirit. He could've lived this life without this dependence, but He chose to live this way in order to prove that we, the human race, can in fact live lives of holiness. We can become better, more human even, if we succumb to a life of dependence on the Holy Spirit. This life comes to us by His power; Jesus even told His disciples to wait for the Holy Spirit because His role in their lives was that important. Theologians call this idea of betterment or living more of holy life, *sanctification.*

Millard J. Erickson's book, *Introducing Christian Doctrine,* defines sanctification as *"The continuing work of God in the life of the believer, making him or her actually holy."*[20] I like this definition because it is easy to understand and because it is sound when it states, *"the continuing work of God."* It's not a one-stop shop when it comes to holiness. We don't just say, "God make me holy," and then it's done forever, as some Christians pretend. We are not made perfect in the sense of total perfection until Heaven. Salvation comes quickly, and we are set apart and considered regenerated, blameless before God and recipients of eternal life—but not 100% holy. There is a moment of being holy and set apart, but there is also a continuing deeper reality to it. A.B. Simpson, in his book *The Fourfold Gospel,* describes it this way: "Many Christians are converted and stop there. They do not go on to the fullness of their life in Christ, and so are in danger of losing what they already possess."[21] Paul talks about this deeper life in Hebrews 10:12:

But when this priest had offered for all time one sacrifice for sins, he sat down at the right hand of God. Since that time he waits for his enemies to be made his footstool, because by one sacrifice he has made perfect forever those who are being made holy.

Paul says, "Those who are being made holy," meaning that sanctification is a perpetual event in the life of the believer. We are made perfect by the sacrifice of Christ, but we are forever being made holy.

---

20   Ibid.
21   A.B. Simpson, *The Fourfold Gospel* (Camp Hill: Christian Publications), 26.

LIVING TRULY TRANSFORMED

Being separate (or different) is what the holy life of sanctification is all about. Those who believe in the saving work of Jesus are set apart from that which previously held them in bondage. We are no longer a part of the "sinners," but we are now "saints"—do they (we) sin? Yes, but our identity has been set apart from the rest of the world because the blood of Christ has regenerated our souls. God, in essence, at the point of salvation picks us up and moves us, setting us apart. The "world" can be defined as those without salvation, those who have not accepted Christ as their Savior. We have been set apart from them; we are different and utterly changed from having to live lives of sinfulness. We are instantly different, but we still have a lot of work to do.

Sadly, many people who follow Jesus forget that they aren't perfect and they don't remember the depths from which they were saved. They pretend to be holy but aren't allowing the Spirit to continue His work in their lives. Sometimes we choose not to be set apart by our actions. In those moments of sin, we are not acting like one who has been set apart. A.B. Simpson puts emphasis on the "being set apart" feature in his book, *Wholly Sanctified,* saying: "The aim and motive must be separated from *all* that is not for His glory; the source of its pleasure must be purified and the spirit separated from all joy that is not in harmony with the joy of the Lord."[22] Simpson then goes on to ask the reader, "Is your spirit separated, cleansed and detached from everything that could defile or distract you from the will of God and life of holiness?"[23]

He asks a tough and searching question. Are we allowing this separation that God so desires to work in us? This shows that we have a part to play in sanctification; God again gives His creation the freedom of choice. We can choose sanctification or not, which is an act of love by our Father. He desires us to be wholly sanctified, yet asks us if we

---

22   A.B Simpson, *Wholly Sanctified: Living a Life Empowered by the Holy Spirit (Camp Hill: Christian Publications),* 28.

23   Ibid.

want it. To me, that is amazing! I am not talking about the instant sanctification that comes at salvation; I am talking about the second mode of sanctification that is the progressive sanctification. We can choose to remain as we are, using salvation merely as "fire insurance" instead of allowing God to completely transform us. Too often, many Christians live this way and don't embrace the reality of the Spirit's work within them. Jesus sent the Spirit so we can be made holy, so we can become better people—yet too often we neglect this deeper working. We choose rather to attempt making ourselves better, and each time find ourselves lacking the ability to do so; there needs to be a deep dependence on His ability to make us better. Then and *only* then can we truly be the better *us* we were meant to be.

Here is another kind of issue that is raised by the idea of us choosing this separation: sometimes we feel that the sanctification is through and by us because we chose it. It can cause a type of "spiritual arrogance" that God never intended. I love A.B. Simpson's book *Wholly Sanctified* because he goes to the core of true sanctification, missing nothing. On this issue of spiritual arrogance Simpson says, "We choose to be transformed to His image, but we cannot create that image by our own morality or struggles after righteousness. We must be created anew in His likeness by His own Spirit, and stamped with His resemblance by His heavenly seal impressed directly upon our hearts from His hand."[24] Every time I read Simpson I can truly see the God-given wisdom that he possessed. It's *only* by the hand of God that we are sealed and made into His resemblance. We cannot make ourselves holy, or better, only *He* can.

When I picture salvation and sanctification, I always think of the nail-pierced hands of Christ. In one of my classes at college, I heard someone describe an image of salvation and sanctification that I will never forget: when we accept Christ in our lives, Jesus goes before His Father, raises His nail-pierced hands on our behalf and says, "I bought that one, and here's the proof." When we choose to accept His

---

24   Ibid.

sanctification, He again goes before His Father and says, "I am setting that one apart for Your glory, I have purchased and ransomed them. They have chosen to be separated by Our Spirit and here is the proof" to which He would then raise His nail-pierced hands again. That picture reminds me that it is *only* through Jesus' death and resurrection that I am both saved and sanctified. I can only be made holy, because He laid down His life in order for His holiness to be spread to me.

This image is why the members at our church plant felt compelled to implement a weekly communion. I believe fully that the communion table serves as a reminder for our hearts and minds that we owe everything to the death and resurrection of Christ. Scripture challenges us to partake of communion, and we are constantly reminded in community, as we remember the cross each week, that we can't do any of it apart from the cross. When I was called to plant a church on the campus of the University of Pittsburgh, I felt compelled to end each sermon with the communion table for this very reason—reminding myself and the congregation that it is *only* through Christ that we can do anything the Word calls us to. If we leave church with a sense of, "OK, I need to do this, I can do this by myself and I will be better," we miss the totality of Christ's narrative.

WE CAN'T DO IT ALONE

The reality of the cross and my dependence upon the Spirit brings a sense of security to me, because I *know* that I am not able to make anything or anyone holy, much less myself. Having God tell me that there is nothing I can do to make myself holy comes as a relief. I know that He is not expecting me to make myself holy and am relieved because I know I'm not alone in my walk with the Lord. I am enfolded by His love, His holiness, and His purity in this walk. I am not left to fend for myself, but He will fend for me. This by no means insinuates that I can be lazy in my walk with the Lord, because the Scriptures call us to be on our guard against Satan and reminds us continually that we need to choose this sanctification daily. Luke 9:23-24 says, "And he said to them all: 'If anyone would come after me, let him deny himself and take up his cross daily and follow me. For whoever would save his life will lose it, but whoever loses his life for my sake will save it.'" I believe that this is a verse about choosing sanctification, as well as simply being a believer in Christ, because I think we have to daily choose to be separated by our God. Due to God's extreme, wild love for us, He daily gives us the choice to walk with Him in this road of sanctification, and so we constantly have to take up our cross and follow Him.

Sanctification has everything to do with the person and life of Jesus Christ. It is *only* through Christ that sanctification is possible, due to His life, death, resurrection, and ascension. Romans 6:4-6 says:

> We were buried therefore with him by baptism into death, in order that, just as Christ was raised from the dead by the glory of the Father, we too might walk in newness of life. For if we have been united with him in a death like his, we shall certainly be united with him in a resurrection like his. We know that our old self was crucified with him in order that the body of sin might be brought to nothing, so that we would no longer be enslaved to sin.

Sanctification begins with Christ as our Savior. Without His death on the cross, the idea, or the thought of sanctification is impossible because we cannot make ourselves holy (as said before). His death is the beginning of sanctification, because we are one with Christ in His death (as said in Romans). When we are baptized, it is not just a symbolic sacrament of the faith; it is vital to our sanctification, because we are publicly declaring our oneness with the Lord. When we are immersed in the water, we are saying essentially that my old self is dead and buried, just as Christ died and was buried. We are becoming one with Him in His death. Without embracing His death as our old self's death, we are not embracing sanctification, because our old self must die.

Thus, if we are one with Christ in His death, we are also one with Him in His resurrection. This is *great* news, because the body of sin has been done away with, and we are no longer slaves to the sin we were once enslaved to! This is the beginning work of sanctification. Sin must first be done away with before we can truly embrace the idea of sanctification. Philippians 3:7-11(NASB) adds a lot to this idea:

> But whatever things were gain to me, those things I have counted as loss for the sake of Christ. More than that, I count all things to be loss in view of the surpassing value of knowing Christ Jesus my Lord, for whom I have suffered the loss of all things, and count them but rubbish so that I may gain Christ, and may be found in Him, not having a righteousness of my own derived from the Law, but that which is through faith in Christ, the righteousness which comes from God on the basis of faith, that I may know Him and the power of His resurrection and the fellowship of His sufferings, being conformed to His death; in order that I may attain to the resurrection from the dead.

These verses reiterate everything I have been saying about Christ as Sanctifier up until this point. We have nothing to offer in this, except that of choosing it, but it is solely by His death and resurrection that we can gain this sanctification. The righteousness we attain, this setting-us-apart-type righteousness, comes only through faith.

COMPLETE SANCTIFICATION

This then leaves the idea: how is the believer then identified with the ascension of Christ? We know how we're identified with Him in His death and resurrection, but how about the ascension? Christ says He will raise up His people into Heaven when He comes again. Full sanctification will happen in that day we are lifted up into Heaven and re-united with Jesus. The fall in Genesis 3 has caused our relationship with the Lord to be hindered. We don't always look to Him to find out who we are; we don't always seek His approval. Because of the fall, we try to find love and acceptance in other places, which causes our human heart to sin. We don't always choose the path of righteousness, nor do we always choose to daily become separated from the world and brought into the fold of God's ever-holy presence, which develops our own holiness.

When we are whisked away from this world and re-united with Him in Heaven, sanctification will be complete. We will no longer need to continuously be made holy, but when we reach Heaven, we will be fully holy as He is holy and this is only through Christ's death, resurrection, and ascension! Our death is the beginning of true life, life as God originally intended for man in the Garden of Eden. This holiness was achieved in Adam, but he chose to walk away from it. Christ (the second Adam) became a sacrifice for us that we might be able to attain what was originally intended for us.

We become like Christ in all our facets only at our own ascension. Then and only then will we be 100% like Christ. That is the true gift of His death, the receiving of full holiness for all of eternity! We will no longer look to earthly things to fulfill us, but God and God alone will we look to for our fulfillment! It is a remarkable thing to think and dwell on, this idea of sanctification and that the fullness of it is ours at our death. For Jesus says in Matthew 16:25b, "Whoever loses his life for my sake will find it." This thought brings much hope and encouragement to the believer because this also shows us how NOT about us it really is. We can't take ourselves into Heaven, we can't give ourselves eternal life, only God can do that, only *He* can fulfill us!

I read a great passage of Scripture recently, which *hit* me like a Mack Truck: "In him you also, when you heard the word of truth, the gospel of your salvation, and believed in him, were sealed with the promised Holy Spirit, who is the guarantee of our inheritance until we acquire possession of it, to the praise of his glory" (Eph. 1:13-14). The Holy Spirit has *many* roles in the life of a believer, and especially in sanctification; however this verse hit me hard. Here, God is saying essentially: "Who the Holy Spirit is and all the stuff that He does for us, is just a down payment on what is to come in Heaven. He is just a deposit proving to you that you are sealed in *me*. The Holy Spirit is just the beginning of your inheritance!"

When Christ was predicting His death and even after His death, He talked of the One who would come after Him, allowing us to do greater things on earth than even He did while He was here on earth! When we choose the sanctification that God has for us, it is the Holy Spirit who comes into our own spirit and transforms us on a daily basis. He is the intercessor for us at the throne of grace. Without the Holy Spirit, we would not be able to understand, comprehend, or even talk to God. It is the Spirit who illuminates our way to God, and highlights His Word and ways.

THE ROLE OF THE HOLY SPIRIT IN SANCTIFICATION

Without the Holy Spirit, who was sent after the death and resurrection of Christ, we would not be able to live holy lives, for He is the very presence of God living within us. I know I've mentioned this before, but it must be re-iterated. We can be and are sanctified even as Christ was sanctified because, and *only* because, we have the same Spirit that led Him in His life here on earth. Christ, while on earth, lived not in His deity, but in His humanity. He led us as an example of how we can be completely surrendered to the Spirit, allowing him to sanctify us daily as he did with Jesus. A.B. Simpson has a lot to say on this subject in *Wholly Sanctified:*

> In the dwelling of the Holy Spirit, we have God's fullness. He has given us the very same Spirit that dwelt in Him. . . . Peter says in connection with the gift of Pentecost that Christ "has received from the Father the promised Holy Spirit and has poured out what you now see and hear" (Acts 2:33b).[25]

---

25 Ibid.

It is *by* the death and resurrection of Christ, but it is *through* His Holy Spirit that we receive the sanctification promised. In my life, I have seen Christ the Sanctifier in my daily walk with Christ. When I accepted Christ at the age of three, I was just doing it out of fear of Hell. However, when I grew up, so did my thinking and reasoning for my belief in Jesus. After my parents' divorce and my mom's struggling second and third marriages, I realized that my faith needed to be something I was sold on, not just my parents' faith, but my own. It was then that I began to understand sanctification. I had to decide to accept the Spirit moving in me, or not.

I chose to surrender to the Spirit and my life has never been the same. I still don't choose sanctification every day, but when I do, my life is always changed. I realize things about God I never knew and realize more about what holiness is. However, the really funny thing is, the more the Spirit reveals to me, the more I realize I don't know. The more righteous I allow the Spirit to make me, the more I truly realize how fallen I am. Jesus is good, because He makes us better—He makes us holy!

REFLECTIONS ON "JESUS MAKES US BETTER"

1. Why would the idea of sanctification be important?

2. Why is the fact that "it's a process, not a once and done deal" matter to you personally?

3. What's the hardest part about surrendering to the Holy Spirit?

JESUS IS A HOLISTIC HEALER

HEALING HAS BEEN A MUCH-DEBATED topic in the history of Christianity. Questions such as "Is it for today?" come up often in discussions of healing. Other questions surface as to the reliability of some physical healings. We, in our human thinking, in many ways can't fathom healing happening the way it did in the Bible. Some doubt so heavily that they simply say, "Healing is not for today; it was for back then," because they can't reason within themselves how it could possibly be for today.

We again return to the main question of this entire book and that is: What good is Jesus? In our broken, sick world, what good is He? Wasn't He just a feel good person that people relied on back then? Why do we need Him now? I will tell you: Jesus is good because He is a holistic healer. He can and does heal physically, emotionally, and spiritually. No other religious system can make such a claim. No pop-culture self-help books can either. Only Jesus ever dared make this claim, and He's backed this claim up by a ton of evidence. What does this look like then? What are some important aspects of healing? How is Jesus able to claim (and do) this holistic healing?

PRAYER AS A MEANS TO HEALING

An important aspect of healing is prayer, in fact it maybe one of the *most* important. Prayer is a powerful tool that believers possess! The Scriptures are full of references on the power of prayer, the direction of prayer, the purpose of prayer, and the sheer connection to God that prayer brings. James is among the books of the Bible that describes prayer. James also connects the act of prayer to healing.

Is anyone among you sick? Let him call for the elders of the church, and let them pray over him, anointing him with oil in the name of the Lord. And the prayer of faith will save the one who is sick, and the Lord will raise him up. And if he has committed sins, he will be forgiven. Therefore, confess your sins to one another and pray for one another, that you may be healed. The prayer of a righteous person has great power as it is working (James 5:14-16).

These few verses are extremely important to understanding Christ as our Holistic Healer. They are also extremely important for those who lead Christ's church in how they are to use healing in today's churches. The fact that Christ is a healer is indisputable, due to His many miraculous healing encounters. Jesus, in John 14:12 stated: "Truly, Truly I say to you, whoever believes in me will also do the works that I do; and greater works than these will he do, because I am going to the Father." The question for us today then is how do we do "even more than He did"? I believe the answer lies here in James 5.

Erickson, an excellent theologian, describes prayer in his book *Introducing Christian Doctrine*: "Prayer does not change what He [God] has purposed to do. It is the means by which He accomplishes His end. It is vital then, that a prayer be uttered, for without it the desired result will not come to pass."[26] Later, Erickson says that prayer "is not a method of creating a positive mental attitude in ourselves so that we are able to do what we have asked to have done. Rather, prayer is in large part a matter of creating in ourselves a right attitude with respect to God's will."[27]

So, when we are praying, we are not "tricking" God into doing what we want, *we are simply positioning ourselves so we can receive fully what He wants*. The same is with the prayer of healing. When the elders pray for a member (the spiritual covering of a member), they are positioning

---

26   Millard J. Erickson, *Introducing Christian Doctrine* (Grand Rapids: Baker Academic, 2001), 144.

27   Ibid.

themselves and the member to receive whatever God has for them. God's answers may vary from "I will heal now" to "It is more merciful of me to allow him to die of this illness." He also may say, "I will heal in My time" or "I will begin healing now and continue the healing."

THE HEALING POWER OF FAITH

James calls the members of the church to go to their elders for prayer as an act of submission and faith, so they can better position themselves to receive whatever God would desire for them to receive. This idea of faith is an amazing part of God's healing and is very similar to the types of healing that Christ did on earth. Jesus was constantly quoted as saying, "Your faith has healed you," or statements very similar. If a member were to follow these verses, the elders would be right in saying, "Your faith has healed you," because they, in faith, brought the matter before their elders in such a way that they were positioning themselves to receive the healing God desired for them. We must not relegate all healing prayer simply to the elders or pastor however. God can and will use each and everyone who believes in Him to be bringers of His healing. A pastor or an elder has no more access to the throne room of God and therefore His healing than any other believer. We must first come in faith to the believer who is praying for the healing.

Had they not had such faith, God may or may not have healed them, just as Jesus didn't heal those in the crowd that did not seek Him out. Keith Bailey in his book *Divine Healing: The Children's Bread* puts it this way: "No limitations were placed on His [Jesus'] healing ministry on earth. Unbelief was the only recorded hindrance to healing."[28]

This also is where James 5:16b that states, "The prayer of a righteous man is powerful and effective" (NIV), comes in. A righteous man will always be seeking to position himself rightly with the Lord, which is why he is considered righteous! He will be praying for the Lord's will to come about! The example that the Scripture gives of Elisha is

---

28   M. Keith Bailey, *Divine Healing: The Children's Bread* (Camp Hill: Christian Publications,1977), 101.

due to his righteous plea, that God show Himself to Israel, and Elisha prays that God will do this in shutting off the rain. This is a righteous prayer, because Elisha was positioning himself to receive what God had for him; God desired to reveal Himself, Elisha just prayed how God would do it!

Let me also say that God can and will heal however and whenever He wants! James 5 is by no means a "box" for the healing of Christ! I have seen numerous healings and heard of healings from friends of mine that definitely happened outside of the elders praying for the infirm of their flock! I will get into that a little later.

First though, one cannot talk about James 5 and not mention the two other huge aspects which bring about the healing God desires for us. The first is the anointing of oil by the elders, and the second is the confession of sins.

THE ANOINTING OF OIL FOR HEALING

The anointing oil goes back to the beginning of the Old Testament. We see the idea first appear in Exodus, in which the priests are supposed to be bathed in this oil in order to set them apart for the ministry that God called them to. Exodus goes on to tell how the oil is made, what goes into it, the amounts etc. It is a part of the consecration process for Aaron and all the priests that follow him (Exodus 30:22-33).

If we will be cut off from all people by putting this oil on anyone other than a priest, why would God ask the elders to anoint the sick with oil? I believe that after the death of Christ, when the temple curtain ripped and tore down the middle, this is another aspect of God's commandments that "changed." The oil, as was stated before, was a symbol of consecration. It meant admitting that I need covering; it was the covering of God! As I study this concept, I see a great correlation to the anointing oil and the Holy Spirit, which was sent to us *after* Christ's death. He mentions the correlation of the Holy Spirit's arrival to Christ's own death several times (John 14,15, and 16). I believe that the anointing oil is symbolic of the Holy Spirit covering the person who has sought out prayer, consecrating them to the will of the Lord. Further positioning them for the will of God to come about in their lives. Keith Bailey, in his book *Divine Healing: The Children's Bread*, says, "The anointing oil symbolizes the direct and immediate work of the Holy Spirit. The Spirit, not the oil, gives life to the body."[29] Also coming to the elders doesn't say that the elders are more holy or that they are sages or healers, but when the elders pray and position themselves and the church member before the Lord, the Lord receives the glory!

THROWING AWAY THE OBJECTS OF OUR SIN

The second huge aspect about healing in James 5 is the confession of sins. If we are sick, we're supposed to call the elders so they can also pray for us. However, we not only have to admit this sickness to God, and ourselves but to the elders of the church, so they too can pray on our behalf. Verse 15b gives both hope as well as a shock. Here it says that the sick person will become well with the prayer of faith but it also says: "if he has committed sins, he will be forgiven." The shock here is that the Scripture says that this malady may have been caused due to sin. I'm not saying that all illness is a result of sin, but I am saying for a fact that sin can and sometimes will cause you to become sick. We also see this in Matthew 9:2 when Jesus heals a sick person but doesn't just say, "Okay, now your body is better," but He also says, "Now your sins are forgiven!" This concept brings our health into a whole new perspective doesn't it? It, to me, says that *God cares more about the healing of my soul than the healing of my body,* and in fact they may coincide with one another! Verse 16 goes even deeper in the first portion: "Therefore, confess your sins to one another and pray for one another, that you may be healed." The "therefore" is saying: since you now know that sin can also cause sickness and prayer can cause healing, confess to each other as well as pray for each other so that you may be healed! This is *true* healing, both body and soul.

---

29   M. Keith Bailey, *Divine Healing: The Children's Bread* (Camp Hill: Christian Publications, 1977), 138-139.

Prayer is important, because we are getting God involved in the fight; we're saying, "I can't do it alone." When we get the elders to pray for us as well, we're saying, "I need help even praying." Confession is important because it exposes our sin and the objects of our sin so God can throw them away. Take for example Jesus at the temple courts (Matt. 21:12-17). He has just entered Jerusalem when He goes to the temple courts and sees people buying and selling offerings. Jesus is totally ticked; He begins to throw the tables saying that they have made God's house a den of thieves. This is a scary part of Scripture, because it changes our view of God and Jesus. We think He's totally peeved at the people and wishes He could throw them, but chooses the tables instead. Rather, Jesus throws the *objects* of their sin. I think He's mad at the deceiver. He hates the sin, and His anger burns against the sin. He displays His utter hatred of the sin to the sinners by throwing the table. I can hear Him saying: "This is *not* what God wants for His house, and this is *not* what God wants for you! So let Me just get this out of your way!"

When we confess to one another, we are exposing our sins and the objects of our sin—the computer, the TV, the phone, whatever it may be—we're exposing it so God can throw it away and say: "This is *not* what I want for your life!" Guess what? We don't have to deal with our problems alone anymore. We have a brother or a sister to fight alongside of us and wrestle with the sin, because God put people in our lives to help us. However, help can only come if we decide to expose our sin. We can expose our sin to God, but we have no earthly accountability and will eventually slip back into the unhealthy pattern. *God desires to heal both body and soul*!

I could continue to harp on this idea of confessing our sins to one another, not only in the context of healing or to only our elders, but as a continual practice with our brothers and sisters. Confessing to others creates a transparent, authentic atmosphere where we can come to better know others, ourselves, and God. I think so much of this concept that I wrote a book on the topic called *Pinocchio Vs. The*

Real Boy which is deeply rooted in 1 John 1:5-2:14. *It is a point of healing that I think the church as a whole overlooks,* yet it is right in the middle of a passage we often use to teach about healing! When we confess our sins to one another, we receive not only fellowship (1 John 1), but healing (James 5)!

THE ROLE OF THE LOCAL CHURCH IN HEALING

What does this all translate to for healing ministry in the local church? The local church should definitely hold to the Scriptures that lay out how we should practice such healing. However, there are still the miraculous healings of the unsaved that need to be addressed. The people Jesus healed were, more often than not, unbelievers with a "faith-inkling" that He could help. They cried out for healing and received it. The church should be the catalyst for such healing! If the church isn't willing to heal the ailing saved *and* unsaved of the world, where will they get such healing? They won't. Bailey talks about the two types of healing available to the world: the "Children's Bread" (part of the atonement and a mercifully generous gift from God to His children) and the miraculous healings of the unsaved.[30] I am totally on board this line of thinking. These two categories should be the focal points of healing for the church. God has some amazing healing for us, both physically and emotionally. We need to seek God, position ourselves, and get ready for His amazing healing.

When discussing healing, the church should focus more on the power of emotional healing because emotions are so intrinsic to the whole person. I touched on this idea when I was talking about the importance of authenticity in our sharing of sins to the elders and other believers, but I didn't make a direct connect yet to emotional healing. Emotional healing is an essential part of healing for the church due to the fact that there are some hurting people that don't think about asking for healing. They may not seem "sick" in the sense we would

---

30 Ibid.

automatically think, yet they are emotionally sick. Part of the local church should focus on dialoguing about emotional health and getting people both saved and healed of their emotional sickness. I have had many encounters with Christ as healer. I will begin with my own personal touch with this type of healing, and then I will discuss what I've *seen* when it comes to healing.

EXPERIENCING INNER HEALING

Several years ago, I went through a class called Personal Spiritual Formation, led by Ron Walborn, at Nyack College. Upon entering the semester, I thought I was a pretty well-put-together individual. Sure, I had problems, but I was okay. When I was in the middle of the semester, God exposed a *ton* of my emotional sicknesses. I realized that I was sick and needed to grieve the pains of my past, confess my issues, and ask my brothers and sisters to pray for healing over me. Long story short, God *did* heal my emotionally wounded heart! I was transformed by His touch, a new creation ready to help others who don't realize the sickness of their own hearts. I can't describe in words what God did for me that semester. All I can describe is only the fact that I knew I was healed; I was prayed over by Ron and others to receive what God had for me. Shortly after, I grew hungry for His Word, reading the Bible, pouring over commentaries for fun, and delving into inspirational books written by authors like Lucado, Kimball, Nouwen, Chesterton, Miller, and many more! I also began to write again, something I hadn't done in years. I even began writing *Pinocchio Vs. The Real Boy,* which was published. God healed me tremendously and in ways I didn't even expect.

The healing that I have *seen* is also pretty incredible. The summer after my sophomore year in high school, I headed to the Amazon jungle in Peru for a month. There are numerous things that happened there that I could share, but this one is probably the best. We were in a medium-sized village, planning our next service, when the speaker for the night, Vince, became very sick. He was throwing up and having the runs all day long. He couldn't stand, much less speak. We tried to get him medicine and something good for his stomach to drink, but nothing seemed to work. No one knew what to do. He was shut up in his tent and just wanted to be left alone. All the sudden, it dawned on my friend Curt to pray for healing for Vince. We all said that it couldn't hurt, so we gathered around Vince's tent. We asked Vince if he would want us to pray for healing. He said, "Yea sure, I guess." So we began to pray. After we were done praying, one of us asked Vince if he believed he was healed and could step out of the tent. Vince didn't say anything, but we heard the zipper on the tent and out walked Vince 100% recovered! That night, he talked about his miraculous healing, and that night many others received the healing of God!

I witnessed another story of healing about my friend Bryan.[31] He received an extraordinary physical healing. For all his life, Bryan had braces on his legs and needed to use crutches to get around everywhere. He'd been praying for healing, and people prayed for healing over and over again for him, but God didn't answer right away. One evening at a healing service, as Bryan was sitting on the floor and praying to God, he heard God say to his heart, "Get up and take off your braces and walk." Bryan said that at first he doubted what was being said to him, but instead of ignoring it, he decided to listen, and if it was wrong, then oh well. Bryan was amazed at what happened! He stood up on his own and walked un-aided for the first time in his life! Not only that, but his feet, which had never felt anything, felt burnt that night in the shower! He felt the heat of the water for the first time.

One more story of healing happened just a few months ago. A new believer in the college church where I am the pastor experienced the love and healing touch of God in one amazing moment. Let me share with you what she said.

Something happened to me this weekend that solidified the love that God has for me. I am not going to lie, it scared me and overwhelmed me, and I am struggling with accepting the love He

---

31   Not his real name

is showing me. Only my mom and Pastor knew about it, but I feel confident that God wants me to share it with all of you:

> On Wednesday at the hospital I saw the tear in my calf muscle. The technician saw the tear. There was a very large tear. I have been in immense pain for almost a month. I was told I would more than likely need surgery to hold the muscle together while it continues to heal. I accepted that. Fine. Whatever. On Friday I read the Bible for the first time in my life. I took notes; I wrote how the words made me feel. It was very intimate for me. I felt calmer about a lot of things—missing my friend's wedding and my gram's birthday party were two of them. I went to bed with a full heart and soul and a calm mind. I prayed that my leg would heal, like I had for the past month, and I went to bed. I woke up in the morning and took a few steps and stopped dead in my tracks. I looked down and started crying. My leg is fine. The bruising is almost gone. The swelling is completely gone and the pain is no more. It's gone. 100% gone. I took my dog for a walk today I even skipped a little. Nope. No pain. God did this. There is no other explanation. This is a miracle. Have a good Sunday.[32]

She just came to know Christ and this incredible thing happened to her! She is a life changed by the power of Christ's healing. In this one healing moment, He captured her heart and healed her physically. I can tell you now that she has *never* been the same. She now works with inner-city kids at our sending church in the inner-city of Pittsburgh. She loves those kids and talks about Christ with them! She has experienced the holistic healing of Christ.

HEALING IS REAL

I know from all the Scriptures and from my own experience that healing is real and for today! God has a desire for us to position

---

32   Rebecca Burns, student at Aletheia Community Alliance Church in Pittsburgh, PA.

ourselves by faith to receive what He has for us. May God continue to heal all of us and allow us to be a healing catalyst to this hurting world! Jesus died in order to set us free holistically: spiritually, physically, and emotionally!

I will end with one aspect of healing; this idea of Jesus being a "Holistic Healer" is the reality of injustice. There is so much brokenness that surrounds us today. Many lives are trapped in sex trafficking, slavery, military subjection, and many other horrific enslavements are alive and well in our world as well. Sadly, many American Christians tend to ignore these realities, but Jesus would not have ignored them. Following the life of Jesus, you see that He made sure to stand up for the least of these. He called others to do so as well. One of His most powerful statements to His disciples and followers was, "Whatever one does for the least of these, has done the same for me,"(paraphrase of Matthew 25:40) meaning that when we serve the poor, broken, and hurting, we are serving Him! One cannot mention Jesus as a holistic healer without discussing His heart to heal the brokenness within systems and governments. One cannot ignore Jesus' passion to help and heal the brokenness within the world around Him. How does He heal this? He sends His people; that's how. Those who believe in His name should be listening to His voice and going out to help serve and heal the brokenness of the people they find. We are the hands and the feet of Jesus. His heart is to be the healer to all the broken and all the hurting, not just the few that show up to church. Jesus is good because He is the Holistic Healer!

REFLECTIONS ON "JESUS IS A HOLISTIC HEALER"

1. What do you most agree with in this chapter? Why?

2. What do you have trouble believing or agreeing with? Why?

3. If the holistic healing of Jesus is true, would you want His healing touch? If so, where?

JESUS IS NOT MONOCULTURAL

WHEN YOU WALK INTO A "monocultural" congregation of Christians, you will generally see an image of Jesus made in their likeness, a Jesus that has their skin tone, hair type, and eye color. I remember a preacher I heard once say: "God made us in His image—let's not return the favor!" Yet we do that, don't we? When we picture Heaven, do you picture a multitude of ethnicities, or does your fantasy reveal a monocultural Heaven? Don't feel ashamed if it's a Heaven that looks just like you, just realize that Heaven will not look the way you've imagined it—Heaven will be filled with many different people, tribes and tongues. This is one lesson I've been learning since the 6th grade when I was living in the inner city of Pittsburgh.

The church where I am blessed to be a pastor, Allegheny Center Alliance Church (ACAC), is an inner-city church with a heart for the city and the inner-city people that dwell within it. This had never seemed more obvious than when an African-American man in the parking lot of McDonald's saw my ACAC van and commented on how we care for all people of different ethnicities. While I was in the drive thru, this spry older gentleman bounded up to my passenger side window and asked one of my middle schoolers (I was then the middle school youth pastor) to roll his window down. The man then struck up a conversation with me for the single purpose of praising ACAC for being not just a multiethnic church, but a multiethnic church that strives to love on all people, no matter the color of their skin. This man I didn't know took notice of our church's dedication to being ethnically diverse. He was happy that there was a church in our community that was dedicated to being a multiethnic center for Jesus to reign. What he was seeing and commenting on was a place that looks like Heaven! He saw Heaven in our church!

ACAC isn't perfect by any means, but we are heading in the right direction and my desire is for us, the church, to have the same passion to be a picture, just a glimpse of Heaven, so that people see that Jesus is good, because He is for all people! People may discriminate against people because of their skin, but Jesus is not like that. He is multicultural! Here is a glimpse of Heaven:

> After this I looked, and behold, a great multitude that no one could number, from every nation, from all tribes and peoples and languages, standing before the throne and before the Lamb, clothed in white robes, with palm branches in their hands, and crying out with a loud voice, "Salvation belongs to our God who sits on the throne, and to the Lamb!" (Rev. 7:9-10).

As I said before, if you thought of heaven with people who look alike (just like you), you've had the wrong picture of heaven your whole life! Jesus died for the *whole* world. Heaven will be made up of all people from all different tribes and tongues. If Jesus is multicultural and Heaven will be looking like a mosaic, why doesn't the church at large look this way? Why is there still so much segregation?

THE MOSAIC TEACHES POWERFUL LESSONS

Think with me of a mosaic picture made up of many different ethnic people. Think of this mosaic as a painting or a tapestry. If it had only one color, wouldn't that be bland? Wouldn't that be boring? Yet, as people who claim to follow the multicultural Jesus, we see way too many bland, one-colored churches.

Without the presence of different types of people, we don't see the full picture! We are made to be together as one body. We all have different gifts, talents, and abilities with which we need to work together (1 Cor. 12:12-14)! We are all different, but the Bible says the same

Spirit links us all. Our picture of Heaven must change; our picture of church must change. When we can work together as one big ethnic mosaic, the *world* will notice! This mosaic picture working together doesn't happen in our world; people hate others of different ethnic backgrounds. People kill people of different ethnicities—these things *still* go on. When we do what God requires of us, being as multicultural as Heaven here on earth, people will notice and desire to know why! The man who purposefully stopped me at McDonald's saw a difference and felt the urge to comment on it. "Why?" one might ask; because it is so strange, so opposite, of many different spaces in our world that it needed to be pointed out. We may live in a world that thinks it's multiethnic, but it is simply fooling itself!

Diversity is something that should happen not only because Heaven will be diverse and because Jesus is multicultural, but also because we as people can learn from people from a different background.

I'm reminded of a film called *Remember the Titans*, where a high school football team in Virginia is integrated. During the season, many hardships force the young men to learn from each other, to accept each other, and to work together as one unit. They grow as individuals and as a team. We can all learn new things from people of different backgrounds, ethnicities, and cultures. We simply have to be like Jesus and attempt to know and reach out to people different than ourselves.

LEARNING FROM DIVERSITY

And he said to them, "You yourselves know how unlawful it is for a Jew to associate with or to visit anyone of another nation, but God has shown me that I should not call any person common or unclean (Acts 10:28).

Directly before this scene in Acts 10, we see Peter wrestling with God about what is good and lawful for him as a Jew to eat. Peter was a good Jewish boy; he didn't eat anything he wasn't supposed to, nor did he hang out with the wrong crowd. He always did the right thing according to Jewish custom. One day, God called him out to go against his culture and get to know a guy who was a different ethnicity than himself. This guy, Cornelius, ate pigs for dinner and had meats that Peter had never even smelled cooking in his house (because he wasn't supposed to), and God asked Peter to go hang out for a meal at this soldier's house. Peter thought God was only for him and people like him, but he learned something new from this diverse encounter! It took wrestling with God for Peter to come to this conclusion—and it was no easy task. Peter was so set in what was good and proper for a Jew that God had to show him a vision three times for his thick skull to get it.

In my life, I've seen this reality of learning from folks from different ethnicities play out time and time again. One funny instance had to do with razor bumps on my neck. I know, you're thinking: WHAT?! But trust me, this is real. I had really bad razor bumps on my neck and face and could never figure out how to cure this ailment in my life. I didn't even know what to call them. I went to all my friends and none of them had any clue what was wrong with me—most thought it was user error. One day my wonderful friend Nate, a biracial brother of mine, finally spoke out. He looked at my neck one day and asked me point blank why I never took care of my razor bumps. I grew excited at his question. "You know what these are?" I asked as I pointed to my very red and nasty-looking neck. He assured me he knew what the problem was and told me that most black men have the same issue. I was dumbfounded! He then prescribed a cream called "Magic: For Black Men Only." I began to use the stuff—it truly was MAGIC! My face stopped looking like a pincushion, and I began to have normal skin again.

I know that's a bit of an odd story, but I learned how to take care of my face better through Nate—and it's all because of his ethnic background. I've had this problem for *years,* and he was the only person who helped me out because none of my white brothers had any idea what was wrong with my face. We can learn much more from each other than just silly things like this, however. We can learn how to worship God and pray differently, taste different foods, experience flavors of life, and discover new things about God from each other. And we can learn a ton about ourselves from people different from us! Once we immerse ourselves with people different from us, it is really shocking all that we can learn about every facet of life.

Don't ever think your way is the only way or the best way! Just like my ways of taking care of my neck weren't the best way, some of the ways we approach and see God are not the best way. Getting to know people of different ethnicities helps the mosaic of our understanding of God to grow too! It's amazing what you can learn from someone who grew up completely different from you. How then do we go about learning from the multicultural Jesus? How then do we interact with those different from us? When asking "What good is Jesus?" we must see that He offers us examples of how to do the things we are now saying He is "good for."

When one looks at the life of Jesus, one can easily see several places where He purposefully interacts with those that are vastly different from Himself. One example is the Samaritan woman (John 4:1-45) with whom He meets at a well and strikes up a conversation. Right from the beginning of this story, we notice Jesus is different. Here, we see something that is quite shocking: the verse states that Jesus *had* to go through Samaria, as if there were no other way. Yet this is not the case. Geographically there were at least two other ways in which Jesus could have gone. One of those ways would completely go around Samaria entirely. This would lengthen the trip quite a bit, but many devout Jews took this route because they perceived the Samaritans as dirty and unclean. If Jews interacted with Samaritans, Jews believed they became dirty until they could cleanse themselves—so "good" Jews ignored Samaria. Jesus intentionally planned to go to Samaria and purposefully struck up a conversation with the woman. There was severe racial tension between these two races, yet Jesus was intentional to break those barriers down. So in order to do the same, we must *be intentional* as well.

When we do things with *strictly* "our group" or people "like us," we hinder what God would desire for us to do. Just like a McFlurry needs to be made on purpose (it doesn't just magically blend), we need to blend with each other to make the heavenly mosaic on purpose. We can't just throw different people together and make them blend; the people in that group have to work at purposefully blending together, there must be intentionality in this.

In the intentional blending of a McFlurry, there is a purpose: to taste delicious. So it is with the intentional blending of people from different backgrounds; they as a whole will taste better to the world around them. So, how do we live with intentionality? I think 1 Corinthians 9:19-22 gives some really great insight. This list is taken from a book, *Ethnic Blends*, which is an amazing book focusing on creating a space for multicultural blending (I highly recommend it). *Ethnic Blends* gives a list of actions you can take to become more ethnically aware:

> You must surrender your preferences.
>
> You must extend yourself to others (those like you and those unlike you).
>
> You must care more for others.[33]

When we add these three portions of intentionality to our lives, we can see the beauty of a multicultural mosaic that will blow your mind!

We should be a people focused on others before ourselves. Jesus was such a person, as we have seen; He hung out with people He "shouldn't have" because He cared more about them than He did anything else, even His reputation. Another challenging way of moving forward with the idea of diversity is by *dropping stereotypes.*

---

33   Mark DeYmaz, *Ethnic Blends: Mixing Diversity Into Your Local Church* (Grand Rapids: Zondervan, 2010), 158-162.

DROPPING STEREOTYPES

The apostle Paul continually called the church to see themselves as equal, mutually bound-together slaves of Christ and servants of one another. Through our faith in Christ, we overcome the boundaries that separate people—whether race, gender, or class. Paul wrote, "There is neither Jew nor Greek, there is neither slave nor free, there is no male and female, for you are all one in Christ Jesus" (Gal. 3:28). We can't be one in real life when we hold negative stereotypes of the people that look or act differently around us. We all have stereotypes for different people. We have ideas of what that person is like without even knowing him or her, simply because of skin color or ethnic background. In order for us to be an ethnic mosaic, we must drop these stereotypes, but how?

So what can we unify around? A Christ-follower's identity is wrapped up in "Christ first." If we see our identity as Christ first, we hold on to what we have in common and leave room to appreciate our differences. This isn't easy. Our challenge is to build fellowship among and between male, female, slave, free, prep, metal-head, Presbyterian, Baptist, old, young, and etc. I believe the breakthrough begins by seeing our fellow followers through a Christ-first lens. Many of us allow stereotypes to grow because of others' experiences, media hype, or from one bad interaction in our own lives. We don't allow God to open up our eyes to our own sinfulness in our unrighteous judgment because we have blinders on. Jesus did not allow blinders to interfere with His passionate desire to reach all people. Let us not try and reach people we've ignored either, lest we allow our stereotypes to offend people and turn them away from God.

We come to the question again—what good is Jesus? Jesus is not monocultural. Many religious experiences that happen in one's life will be monocultural, and there will be a racism that goes into many religious experiences—even, I'm afraid, in 'Christian' experiences. Yet, Jesus is not one to hold to a racist attitude. His desire is to see all nations, tongues, tribes, and ethnicities represented in Heaven because

He loves all. We are then to have the same heart and to seek to join hands with those who are different than ourselves, creating a beautiful tapestry built out of a mosaic of people. Let us start now.

In working at a secular university that prides itself on "diversity," I've seen the opposite. Many believe that being diverse means that there is a representative from an ethnicity, not blended, but completely and purposefully other than. For example, there are separate ministries strictly for the Asian, black, and white people on this particular campus. That simply isn't diversity; it's segregation. In Heaven, we won't have different sections of the sanctuary designated Asian, white, black, Latino, and so on. We will be together as one body worshipping one Lord with one voice! Why is it that we segregate out now? May we be people who seek to be one here and now. When everything in our culture tells us to avoid Samaria, may we, like Jesus, follow the leading of the Spirit and go through Samaria rather than around it!

ENGAGE THE TAPESTRY

I believe that many in our country today live under the delusion that race no longer plays a role in our lives as Americans. This delusion shrouds the minds of mostly white, middle to upper class people because those of different ethnicities know too well that race (or as I prefer to call it, ethnicity) plays a significant role here in America. Don't believe me? Imagine yourself as a black man in Missouri.

The reality is, we are still a very segregated and racist culture. Sunday in America is still the most segregated day of the week, which saddens me. It saddens me, because if we are truly going to attack this issue of racism in America, it has to begin with the church. We have to be the model that there is a way to have healthy diversity within a group of people.

Let's take my city of Pittsburgh as an example. This city is a very vast tapestry with many different ethnic backgrounds weaved into it. Pittsburgh houses refugees from Nepal and Africans from many different countries, as well as a wide mosaic of ethnic diversity. Yet, here we silo off. All ethnic groups segregate and stay within their own grouping of people who look and talk like them. What if we decided that a few of us from each ethnic group should come together to experience the tapestry from which we live in?

Many people would declare: "I'm not racist. I just like to be with people of my own culture who understand me and what I go through." I totally get that; I really do. When I moved from Akron, Ohio, to Pittsburgh, Pennsylvania, I understood for the first time what it meant to be in the minority. I attended an inner-city middle school and high school here in Pittsburgh. I remember having that feeling of wanting to be with people who looked like me. Yet as I engaged the tapestry, my desires to be with people only like myself changed. I changed. On my inner-city football squad, then the Northside Saints, I was christened: "Graham Cracker Ca" ("ca" is a shortened version of the word cousin). Although on the outset that may seem racist against me, in many ways it was an honor. I asked my friends on the team, "Why do I have to be a cracker?" They all laughed and declared that Graham Crackers are different from saltines because they have some brown laced in it. It struck me that I have changed. My ethnicity clearly was still a part of me, but I was living well within the tapestry, the beautiful connectedness of different fabrics was taking place in my life. We can segregate completely and be two separate images, or we can be distinctly different yet woven together in the manner of a mosaic tapestry. It's not a fully separate or fully blended reality, when we engage ethnic diversity it becomes a tapestry.

Weaving into a tapestry, rather than being "segregated from," changed my entire life. I began to realize that *white privilege is real*. I began to realize that I had my own racist ideas and wrestled with labels and judgments based off of how someone was dressed. Being weaved in exposed me for who I was: *a racist*. Even though I didn't think I was—I actually was.

I truly believe that this weaving is the only way we can truly break racism in the church and further out into America herself. The ideas of other ethnicities that we all hold to will shatter. The images that we have will crumble. We can learn so much about life, and about ourselves, by weaving and engaging in the tapestry. We will need to make ourselves uncomfortable as we venture down this road, and we'll need to begin to purposely make friends from different ethnicities. But we can't weave into the tapestry without connecting ourselves to others. Racism will never end just by talking about it. People can talk all day long about ending racism, but if they don't do anything, their talking is pointless. Many people feel like "the conversation on race has come a long way," but note it's still a "conversation." That means it's really not gone much of anywhere. Martin Luther King Jr.'s dream wasn't just for the outside of people to change, but rather the inside as well.

When one engages the tapestry of diversity you will find that you know so little about your own ethnicity and about God, art, music, love, language, and life. I was (and still am) amazed at how much I learned (and continue to learn) about all of these things by simply engaging the tapestry of others' ethnicities. Learning comes from not only doing a book study of people from different ethnicities, but living life with them. My knowledge was so plain, so one directional, and still is in many ways. That's why I need the tapestry. God designed it this way. Heaven will be the beautiful mosaic, why not start now? If you imagined Heaven as all-white hipsters playing drums and doing beat poetry, your vision of Heaven is too small. If you imagined Heaven as anything different than a mosaic tapestry of life, you've missed it!

Let's not simply be people who have conversations about racism; let's be people who live differently. Let us all enjoy and engage the vast mosaic picture that God has painted. Let's all be woven into the tapestry of Heaven. It's not a melting pot where we are all blended and miss the ability to be distinctly different, it is our distinctly different selves purposefully attaching our lives to the lives of others who are different as well![34]

---

34   Adapted from: *In REAL Life; "Engage the Tapestry: Thoughts on Ethnic Diversity,"* blog entry by E. Marvin Nelson, October 22, 1014.

WE ARE SNEETCHES

Dr. Seuss has an amazing story called "The Sneetches," which deals with different people learning how to be neighbors. In the land of the sneetch, there are two different types of sneetches—those with stars upon thars (their bellies) and those with none. The sneetches with the "stars upon thars" always live with an air of superiority in the air, as if somehow, the stars made them more worthy of life. The sneetches without stars began to believe the lie as well. Soon, an inventor came into their little town with a machine that could put stars upon thars, and every Sneetch without stars paid the inventor money to be like those with stars. They began to strut about with their new-found assurance of their lives being worth while, and it bothered the previously starred sneetches. The inventor made a new machine that took stars off, so there could be a uniqueness again. The previously starred sneetches began to pay the inventor to take off their stars, and once the stars were off, they walked with their noses in the air as if they now were superior again. The inventor made a boatload of money that day as people kept switching from starred to unstarred until no one knew who was who. After spending all of their money, the sneetches eventually came to the conclusion that a sneetch was a sneetch, no matter what, starred or unstarred.[35]

I tell that story because we as an American nation are fighting a fight we tricked ourselves into thinking was over. We have not realized that a human is a human, no matter his or her skin color. Racism still runs rampant in our society and, worse, in many of our churches. We still find that we live by stereotyping people of a different skin tone than ourselves. We've not learned the lesson of being a neighbor the way Jesus taught it. We've been living a delusional mindset of being over this issue, when there is still a long way to go.

We are not where we think we are when it comes to racism. Many people would even say that Jesus never actually taught on racism, but

---

35   Dr. Seuss, "The Sneetches," *Dr. Seuss and Other Stories,* (New York: Random House, 1961).

they would be wrong. Here in the story of "The Good Samaritan," we see Jesus confronting many Biblical issues at once, including racism. The question we must then ask is, "What does Jesus teach us about racism through being a neighbor?"

> But he, desiring to justify himself, said to Jesus, "And who is my neighbor?" Jesus replied, "A man was going down from Jerusalem to Jericho, and he fell among robbers, who stripped him and beat him and departed, leaving him half dead. Now by chance a priest was going down that road, and when he saw him he passed by on the other side. So likewise a Levite, when he came to the place and saw him, passed by on the other side. But a Samaritan, as he journeyed, came to where he was, and when he saw him, he had compassion. He went to him and bound up his wounds, pouring on oil and wine. Then he set him on his own animal and brought him to an inn and took care of him. And the next day he took out two denarii and gave them to the innkeeper, saying, 'Take care of him, and whatever more you spend, I will repay you when I come back.' Which of these three, do you think, proved to be a neighbor to the man who fell among the robbers?" He said, "The one who showed him mercy." And Jesus said to him, "You go, and do likewise" (Luke 10:29-37).

Here we see a story that doesn't seem to deal with racism at all, but it's packed with tons about that very topic. When looking at this story, we must see Jesus telling us who our neighbor is, and understand that His teachings on being a neighbor highlight our need to let go of our snooty "starred sneetch" mentality. Many times in church we don't deal with this issue within this text, because, as Warren Wiersbe said (of this very parable), "It is much easier to maintain a religious system than it is to improve the neighborhood.[36]" Many times we'd rather

---

36   W. W. Wiersbe, *The Bible Exposition Commentary, Vol. 1*, (Wheaton: Victor Books, 1996), 212.

deal with the "religious" portions of Scripture and neglect the social portions of Scripture. In our neighborhoods, we need more people who see people the way this Samaritan saw people.

BEGIN TO SEE EVERY PERSON AS OUR NEIGHBOR

In using a Samaritan in this story, Jesus goes into deeper issues than the Jews were ready for, namely their racism and its inconsistency with the Scripture. Jesus talked about racism and dealt with it in His life. Here Jesus uses a Samaritan to shame the Jews. The two neighboring communities were completely at odds with each other. They both had a deep-seated hatred for one another, and the Jews labeled the Samaritans as "half breeds" and saw them as "dirty" and unable to worship at the temple along side of them. If Jews came in contact with a Samaritan, they'd consider themselves "unclean." When traveling, they'd purposefully *avoid* Samaria by travelling around it, even though it took longer. Here, a young, arrogant "Bible scholar" tries to trick Jesus into saying the wrong thing, and Jesus points out that the young man fails to live out the entirety of the Law he claimed to "love." The Jews in the story who walked by lacked mercy, lacked sacrifice, and chose themselves above their neighbor, even though they were the people of God. Even though they were the "chosen ones," they neglected to follow the Law by loving their neighbor as themselves. The young guy talking with Jesus had the right answer but the wrong application. This young Jew thought he was living the Law well, and, with a short story, Jesus dismantled his thinking.

Too often, I think even the people of God completely do the same thing when it comes to loving our neighbors. The American church is still one of the most segregated places on Sunday. We too then seem to have a sneetch problem but fail to see it. Reflecting the "starred" sneetches, the Jews in this story thought they were more "human" than the Samaritans, and thus believed that the reality of the Scripture didn't demand they consider the lowly Samaritans as their neighbors. You may not see this, but many white Americans treat people of other skin colors as sneetches without stars, even within the church. The church can and must change this.

Think of recent racial issues going on in our current culture. How has the church's response been as a whole? I'd venture to say it has *not* been united. The one group of people who should be able to stand up together for justice has been segregating itself. There has been little mercy, little tenderness, and a severe lack of judgment in how we speak about these issues. When white on black brutality happens, many white people will say: "that's just a coincidence," while many black people feel it more deeply because it reminds them of the brutality they suffered not long ago. Whether or not the motives in the brutality are the same, the church allows this reminiscent pain and does nothing! Rather than loving the hurting black community, many churches have condemned them for their pain. Granted this is not always the purpose, but it is still the case.

We've not yet arrived at the place of The Good Samaritan in our culture. We are still blind to actually loving our neighbors. We can't pick and choose our neighbor, just as we couldn't choose the culture into which we were born. When we can begin to see every person as the neighbor we need to love as we love ourselves, this world will begin to see the difference God really makes in our lives. No matter one's skin tone, we are called to love and serve our neighbors, not abuse, disown, and leave for dead the people we find broken along the way of life.

Racism hurts the heart of God. It is a spiritual compromise. Earlier this week, in a conversation with Pastor Rock, he stated off the cuff: "In every compromise, we give away a piece of God." God is not about compromising His love for anyone, no matter what the reason. During His earthly ministry, Jesus went out of His way to break racial boundaries.

TO LOVE OUR NEIGHBOR, SACRIFICE IS REQUIRED

The Samaritan deemed this man's life as more important than his schedule. He was clearly going somewhere, yet chose to stop and assist the man. The Jewish men in the story of The Good Samaritan didn't deem this man worth it. They would have needed to cleanse themselves after touching all the blood and they were more than likely on their way to somewhere as well. They decided not to love their neighbor, even though he was of their ethnicity. Yet, this Samaritan, this "dirty dog" as many a Jew would've labeled him, thought less of himself and had compassion. It wasn't a demeaning compassion either. I think too often, we see many having a compassion on people from other ethnicities with a demeaning compassion, a "white-knight" syndrome if you will. This Samaritan was not worried about "being a hero;" he was moved with love and sacrificed his time and his money to care for this man who just lost everything and almost lost his life.

We, too, are called to a level of sacrifice when it comes to our neighbors. In order to love and interact with our multiethnic neighbors, we must be willing to sacrifice preferences, styles, and even some of our "cultural norms." We must also be willing to sacrifice time and make a real effort at getting to know others so we don't find ourselves thinking we are superior or allow our stereotypes to lead us down a path of false judgment. When looking at the Scripture, in particular Philippians 2, we can see that we should count others better than ourselves, because, in His coming into the world, Christ didn't hold on to His superiority. If we were truly to live like Christ, racism, sexism, and classism wouldn't exist because we'd be a people who lacked a superiority complex. Much racism, even in this story Jesus told, stems from an assumption of superiority. If God so loved the world that He stepped down off the throne and let go of His superiority, we should be willing to do the same. Sadly, the American church as a whole has a superiority complex, and that poison spreads throughout the body into racism, sexism, and classism.

Being a good neighbor is seeing everyone as a neighbor, no matter his or her skin tone. We don't become color blind because the mosaic that God made is beautiful, but instead we simply choose not to allow color to cause us to make snap judgments. The Samaritan in the story understands this better than the people of God it was being told to. We choose to walk compassionately alongside our neighbors, not with demeaning compassion, but with sincere love in our hearts for them. When we love others as we love ourselves, we begin to watch out for their best interests, not our own.

Here was my challenge to our college church plant: may we be a people here in Oakland who live seeing everyone as a neighbor and choose to love unconditionally and sacrificially, like the Samaritan Jesus highlighted in His parable. What do we as Aletheia look like? *My desire for us, and I believe God's desire for us, is to see the ethnic makeup of the world around us reflected in our churches on a weekly basis.*

Jesus is good, because He is NOT monocultural. This world needs Jesus, the *real* Jesus. May we be people who bring Jesus to this world and begin to display the mosaic tapestry that He will one day fully display in Heaven!

REFLECTIONS ON "JESUS IS NOT MONOCULTURAL"

1. What idea do you most agree with in this chapter? Why?

2. What concept do you have trouble believing or agreeing with? Why?

3. How often have you "avoided Samaria" because of stereotypes?

4. How can you be more intentional in seeking out friends and Christian brothers and sisters who are ethnically different from you?

5. What have you learned already from some who are different than yourself?

JESUS KEEPS IT REAL

THERE'S A VERY OLD TALE that begins with a pauper. This poor young man must steal to survive. He wanders around the streets, searching for his next victim of thievery; this simply is part of life. The palace guards know him as a "street rat" that has fleas and is despised and hated by the rich and powerful. These harsh realities are his life, yet one day his whole life changes.

While running his daily routine of thievery, he sees a beautiful woman who takes an apple from a market vendor. The vendor is vehemently yelling at this young lady when this street rat rescues her from the vile vendor. He spends the rest of his day with this gorgeous woman, talking to her about his life and his existence and showing her what he believes to be the most opulent thing in his life—his room with a view of the palace. He regales her with his thoughts of living in the palace and how it would be marvelous to have servants who serve you on a whim, mentioning that it would be glorious to have such a life, because his own existence is so horrible.

After his stories and excited talk about servants and palaces, the palace guards enter the scene. They storm into his little hovel and try to grab the young man. The young, beautiful woman steps in, throws off her hood, and demands the young man's release by the order of the princess! This young, gorgeous woman was the princess all along!

Of course this changes everything for the young man, yet he can do nothing about it until, by a change of events, he comes in contact with a genie. He asks this genie to make him royalty so he can be the suitor for the princess. He wants her hand and sees that the only way that he can get her to be his is by lying about who he is. No longer the street rat (because, let's face it, a princess won't and *can't* marry a street rat), he is Prince Ali Ababwa! He shows up at the palace and wins an audience with the princess. She at first rejects him, but then he later convinces her to go on a "magical carpet ride" with him. This is where we see this mask of Ali (which, by the way, is really Aladdin, if you didn't know yet) hitting its stride. The princess Jasmine asks over and over if she has seen him before, because she suspects he is Aladdin, yet he denies it over and over again. Aladdin fears that Jasmine, knowing who he really is, will deny him and treat him as a street rat, the street rat he knows he really is. He was obviously *not* being real about who he truly is. In the end, his rouse hurt him more than it could ever help him. He almost lost the love of his life because he tried to make a mask that would please her, when all along all she wanted the real Aladdin, not the mask he was wearing.

We as human beings suffer from this same problem—hiding our true identity for fear of being exposed. Our masks take over who we are, and we aren't truly known, nor are we real.[37] This problem seems to be much larger with the followers of Christ. There seems to be a belief that if you are a follower of Christ that you must have your act together. However, Jesus was not one for masks, nor did He delight in those who were faking it. Many unsaved people assume that because masks are more normative for Jesus' followers, this was the way in which Jesus lived His life as well. Yet, Jesus kept it real and desires to keep it real still! One of Gandhi's most famous sayings about Christianity is this: *"I like your Christ. I do not like your Christians. They are so unlike your Christ."* I sadly would have to agree with him in many ways, but none so much as the lack of authenticity in Jesus' followers.

Many people, including myself, have walked around in darkness, hiding our sins, our shame, and our doubts for far too long. Jesus is good because He keeps it real. He desires to allow all things to be exposed in the light and not covered in darkness. John was a man who deeply loved Jesus and felt himself deeply loved by Jesus as well, thus he continuously called himself, "the disciple who Jesus loved." When

---

37   Nelson, E. Marv, *Pinocchio Vs. The Real Boy*, (Mobile: Rev Press, 2011), 27-28.

John saw the followers of Jesus living in darkness, he felt compelled to call them back to living in the light. In John's letter (now Scripture) he says:

> This is the message we have heard from him and proclaim to you, that God is light, and in him is no darkness at all. If we say we have fellowship with him while we walk in darkness, we lie and do not practice the truth. But if we walk in the light, as he is in the light, we have fellowship with one another, and the blood of Jesus his Son cleanses us from all sin (1 John 1:5-7).

Here we see John encouraging God's people to not live fake, hypocritical lives, but to instead let all things be exposed by the light. The darkness is not a good place to live; only in the light can we find cleansing of sins. Many people have often said, "God is a gentleman. He won't force Himself upon you," and this statement is very true. He is not going to drag your sins out of the darkness and force forgiveness upon you. He desires for you to bring those things from the dark into the light so He can do the cleansing work you and I need.

Many religious organizations, including the church, tend to cause people to hide their real struggles, fears, doubts, and sins for the sake of fitting in. There is an external pressure to measure up so that, when we are weighed and measured, we are not found wanting. Jesus, however, is opposite because He knows we are not perfect. He knows we have skeletons in our closet and that the only way to be our true selves and live in freedom is to expose all things into the light.

I recently watched the movie *Flight,* with Denzel Washington, which hits this concept perfectly on the head, and the movie's ability to get this concept so well was for me an unexpected twist to the film. To be fair, this film is rated R, so it is not for everyone. However, it goes deep into this particular idea of exposing self to gain freedom. Denzel's character, Whip Whitaker, is a pilot with a drug and alcohol problem. In the opening scenes of the film, we see him drinking a beer in the morning and sniffing cocaine right before he gets on the flight to fly the plane. Then, while on the plane he pours three single serve vodka bottles into his orange juice.

The plane crashes due to malfunctioning equipment, yet Whip was still able to control the plane and cause the safest landing possible. Due to the crash, there was an investigation into Whip, and it is exposed that he had alcohol and drugs in his system. For the entire film, Whip continuously denies having a problem, claiming he could quit anytime. He keeps his drunkenness a secret from the public eye, has his lawyer ensure that the toxicology screen of his blood tossed out, and continues to drink throughout the film. It's not until the very end of the film when he is pushed to his limits in a trial that he admits his struggle and calls himself an alcoholic.

The scene then shifts to him in prison eighteen months later, talking to the other inmates and sharing his whole experience and talking about exposing the lies he had continuously thrown into his life. He lost his wife, his son's respect, his job, and friend after friend due to his addiction because he simply continued to cover it up with lies. Yet, here with these inmates, he confesses how being in jail and being sober for eighteen months has been the greatest experience in his life because as he stated: "I am finally, for the first time in my life, free!" That freedom came from bringing his real issue into the light and not letting it sit in the darkness anymore. In the darkness, he was trapped; he pushed people away and lost countless people from his life, but once he exposed his alcoholism, he was free!

This is the *freedom* that Jesus offers in our confession as well. Jesus keeps it real and knows that only when we expose the darkness in our hearts and life will we experience the freedom He offers! It will be utterly frightening to expose oneself in this way; it sure was for Whip—that's why he hid for so long! Despite the difficulty to bring exposure, it is always worth it to do so. Later in that chapter of I John, John says this of Jesus: "If we confess our sins, he is faithful and just to forgive us our sins and to cleanse us from all unrighteousness" (1

John 1:9). Not only will exposing things in the light bring freedom, but with Christ it brings forgiveness and cleansing that no other religion promises. We don't have to work for or earn this forgiveness or cleansing, we simply need to confess our sins.

Followers of Christ should be the first to jump on this train of confession, but sadly this is not true in many Christ followers' lives. Jesus is good because He keeps it real. When it comes to people who declare themselves faithful, but are hiding in the darkness, He goes to great lengths to challenge them. In Matthew 23, we can see one of Jesus' harsh challenges to the Pharisees who thought themselves to be perfect in the sight of God, and I think we may also see ourselves in this speech by Jesus. Jesus says to these men, "But woe to you, scribes and Pharisees, hypocrites! For you shut the kingdom of heaven in people's faces. For you neither enter yourselves nor allow those who would enter to go in" (Matt. 23:13-14).

Are we, because of our lack of confession and authenticity, hypocrites like these Pharisees whom Jesus condemns? Do we shut the door of the Kingdom of Heaven in people's faces, meaning that by our hypocrisy we don't allow people access to God? From what I've seen, I'm afraid that our churches try to shut people out, which means we have either done the same thing as the Pharisees, commanded it to be done, or sat back quietly as our people did it. Jesus continues a bit later in chapter 23:

> Woe to you, scribes and Pharisees, hypocrites! For you clean the outside of the cup and the plate, but inside they are full of greed and self-indulgence. You blind Pharisee! First clean the inside of the cup and the plate, that the outside also may be clean. Woe to you, scribes and Pharisees, hypocrites! For you are like whitewashed tombs, which outwardly appear beautiful, but within are full of dead people's bones and all uncleanness. So you also outwardly appear righteous to others, but within you are full of hypocrisy and lawlessness (Matt. 23:25-28).

These verses have always personally hit me hard. How often do I clean the outside of my cup, all the while leaving the inside dirty, full of un-confessed sin? To make the picture even more dire and grotesque, Jesus says that the insides of the Pharisees are like dead people's bones! Jesus' heart is for us to stop polishing the outward shell of our lives and ask Him to change our whole self and become real. Like in the story of Whip, it can be easier, and it's definitely simpler, to stay hidden and attached to the lies, but this was not the intent God had for us at our creation. Jesus has harsh words for those who remain hidden and continue to polish the outside, rather than exposing their hearts. He's harsh not because He enjoys being so, but because He desperately wants us to wake up to the reality that staying hidden is a far worse fate than being exposed and healed by Him.

Earlier I likened this idea to a story most people already knew: the story of Aladdin. Most of us have seen the Disney movie that shows this "street rat" become a prince and win the heart of the lady he so loves. Aladdin finds the lamp with the genie inside who will grant three wishes. Because he loves Princess Jasmine, Aladdin desires to no longer be the "street rat" and wishes for Genie to make him a Prince. He then becomes "Prince Ali Ababwa."

Once he becomes this false prince, he becomes arrogant and lies to everyone about who he truly is, even his beloved Princess. As Ali, he and Jasmine have a wonderful carpet ride (when, in the Disney rendition, they sing: "A Whole New World"). The Princess, guessing that she has seen him before, asks him several times if she knows him and whether or not he was in the market place. Aladdin constantly lies, saying that he couldn't have been in the market place. Then changes his mind, saying that he was in the market place, but it was absurd to think that "royalty" would be in the market place spinning a web of lies. Eventually Jafar exposes the lie that this "Prince Ali" is really a nobody, good-for-nothing, street rat named Aladdin.

From the beginning of Aladdin's lie, Genie tries to get Aladdin to be honest about who he really was, and not to lie. However, Aladdin doesn't want to be real with who he was, because he *feared* she would no longer love him, nor accept him.[38] [39] This is exactly how we as Christians sometimes treat our sin by covering up or lying to other believers, ourselves and God. We are afraid to expose our sins because we fear we won't be accepted by our fellow believers, ourselves, or even by God.

This lie is completely from Satan! Sadly, in churches today, if you're struggling with sin, especially what some would consider "*big* sins," you will be judged and no longer accepted, but this is *never* the case with God, and, quite frankly, *should never* be the case with the church!

What happens when we fail to be real with God, others, and ourselves is that we stumble around in the darkness, and this is exactly where Satan wants us to be. Let me urge you to first be real with both God and yourself. This will expose the sin in your life so you can shine light on it and put it behind you. Don't fear rejection from God because *it won't happen.* Also don't shame or guilt yourself, because that will *tear you apart.* I know from personal experience. I am not saying I have it all together, because I don't. I have to constantly urge myself not to do these things as well. I am a people pleaser at heart so I need to constantly tell myself that God is not happy with me because of what I do or don't do but that He loves me for who I am, and that is His beloved son! He doesn't desire me to be stuck in the pit of my own making however. When we confess and are real, laid bare before the Lord, He will change us.

Jesus is good. He keeps it real and so the followers of Christ should keep it real as well. Imagine how those outside the church would look differently at Jesus if they saw the power of His followers being real. The world is asking: "What good is Jesus?" When the world looks at His people and see a pool of fake, masked, hidden

---

38   Jonathan Freeman, Gilbert Gottfried, Linda Larkin, Douglas Seale, Scott Weinger, Frank Welker and Robin Williams. *Aladdin*, DVD. Directed by Ron Clements and John Musker. Burbank, CA: Walt Disney Pictures, 1992.

39   Written about previously: Nelson, E. Marv, *Pinocchio Vs. The Real Boy*, (Mobile: Rev Press, 2011), 27-28.

people, it appears that Jesus actually has nothing to offer. Despite what we've discussed, if His people don't look like Christ, they won't see Christ. In the next chapter we will look at why the church exists, but remember that the people of God are to be the image of God to this world. What do you see in the church? If it's hiddenness, how can you be different?

REFLECTIONS ON "JESUS KEEPS IT REAL"

1. What do you most agree with in this chapter? Why?

2. What do you have trouble believing or agreeing with? Why?

3. How often do you hide in the darkness?

4. What's keeping you from exposing the sin in your life and allowing His healing to come?

5. What is your personal experience with the church and it being "fake"? How can you be different and make a difference?

JESUS WOULD NOT RUN
FOR PRESIDENT

IN MANY YOUNG PEOPLE'S MINDS, Christianity is synonymous with right-wing politics. In their groundbreaking work *UnChristian*, Kinnaman and Lyons discuss their discovery that 46% of young outsiders (16-29 years old) from the church considered the Christians to be too involved in politics and 75% said Christians were involved "a lot" or "some."[40] These were negative feelings, not happy or excited ones. "Being too political" is something these young folks dislike or even despise about Christians. In fact, I am tired of it too because being overly involved in politics has so little Biblical support and serves only to drive people further from Jesus rather than towards Him. I feel this is especially so, because there are two main parties who espouse that Jesus would be for their party and not the other. This creates a very toxic environment and uses Jesus where Jesus ought not to be used.

Politics and faith can go hand in hand; however, to assert that one's political party is much more "righteous in the sight of God" is simply despicable, *un*righteous manipulation. I fear that for many Christians, both conservative and liberal, their political desires have begun to outweigh their Kingdom of God desires; they'd rather see their candidate win and their political agendas upheld then see people come to Christ. They, of course, would deny this reality, but the proof is in the pudding when it comes to their actions. The Christian's *deep* involvement in politics confuses the outsider on who Jesus really is, and really does push people away from Him. If we could divorce some

---

40   David Kinnaman and Gabe Lyons, *UnChristian: What a New Generation Really Thinks about Christianity . . . and Why It Matters* (Grand Rapids: Baker Books, 2007), 28.

of our rhetoric from the political sphere, I think we could do a much better job of showing how Jesus is good.

I remember it like it was yesterday. I was a freshman in college, sitting in Nyack College's cafeteria filling out my PA absentee ballot. Hilary and I were together filling these ballots out so we could help determine the next President of the United States. I loudly declared (as obnoxiously as I could) that I was proudly voting for George Bush and NOT John Kerry. I had recently seen a video on the Internet hilariously calling John Kerry "Satan" because he was of the Democrat persuasion. I shared this video with all my friends and (jokingly) reminded those in earshot that John Kerry was "Satanic." I then enthusiastically, with much flair filled out my ballot and sent it in voting for the *very* republican George W. Bush. In those days of my life, I thought that my Christianity and my political leanings were one and the same. I felt that to be republican was to be Christian and vice versa. I had begun to be as dedicated to my political agenda as I was to the agenda of God. Not long after, I would understand this is not the case. I was an over-politicized follower of Jesus, as I fear many American believers are. Jesus' life told a different story than one of political gain or upheaval. In fact, some would say it was completely opposite. I share this to state that I too have been (and may still falter into) a political Christian.

We live in a highly politicized society. People, both Christians and non-Christians, find deep hate for someone who espouses different political views than themselves. Fights, harsh words, and even wars may start from a disagreement on political issues. We then must ask, "What good is Jesus in the midst of politics?"

JESUS WAS NOT FULL OF RHETORIC BUT RATHER WAS FULL OF ACTION

So they asked him, "Teacher, we know that you speak and teach rightly, and show no partiality, but truly teach the way of God. Is it lawful for us to give tribute to Caesar, or not?" But he perceived their craftiness, and said to them, "Show me a denarius. Whose likeness and inscription does it have?" They said, "Caesar's." He said to them, "Then render to Caesar the things that are Caesar's, and to God the things that are God's." And they were not able in the presence of the people to catch him in what he said, but marveling at his answer they became silent (Luke 20:21-26).

When one looks at the life of Jesus, studies His life and His words, rarely do we see Him interacting with the world of politics. One of the places when He does interact, it's not to defame or deplete the government He is under; but rather to publicly support it!

These men were trying to ensnare Jesus in the political arena and he simply told them to give to Caesar that which belongs to Caesar. He didn't begin to defame Caesar; He didn't jump at the chance to go on and on about the political issues of the day and moved on. If any teacher in history had the right to go on and on about the political issues of his or her day, it was Jesus. He was a Jew trapped in an unjust system of Rome. He was part of a conquered land and Caesar was not the king any Jew wanted to be under; he was pagan after all! Yet, one quickly notices Jesus does not go on and on here but simply and quickly ends the discussion. Here Jesus displays a restraint that was unknown among the rabbis of His day. Many of them would've taken such an open opportunity to remind the Israelites they were oppressed. There were factions in Jesus' day split on the issues of Rome support or Rome destruction. Do not be misled by many political Christians who may state no one in Jesus' day was political, and thus Jesus was not due to this reality, because that is a bunch of lies.

Many followers of Christ desire to tout Him as a political figure, but He wasn't. His involvement in politics was scarce and minimal at best. He didn't come to overthrow Roman government; He didn't come to lead a rebellion to "secure senate seats" in the Empire. He didn't come to even try to supplant the Emperor and "enforce His 'law' upon the people" or come to legislate moralism. He came to seek and save the lost. He came to live and die for all and to challenge His followers to do the same.

We may want a Senator, but Jesus is a Savior. Jesus didn't spend time lobbying for the poor, or developing laws to shut the mouths of the Pharisees. Jesus didn't complain on Facebook about how Caesar was leading or what an "ungodly" king he was. Jesus acted. He lived His belief. In his book *Jesus for President,* Shane Claiborne uses the term "political embodiment" to describe Jesus' actions. Claiborne states that "political embodiment means that we become the change that we want in the world, not just lobby politicians to change things for us. Not many of us have seen people, much less a political party, who are ready to enact the change they want in the world."[41]

JESUS DESIRES OUR HEARTS WHILE POLITICS DESIRES OUR BEHAVIORS (JOEL 2:12-13; MATT. 5:8)

When you look at the book of Acts, the story that chronicles the genesis of the church, you'd figure the most important ways the church can BE the church would be found here. If we were to be deeply politically engaged, I think we would have seen at least traces of that pictured in there for us as an example to follow. Jesus gave us our marching orders: to make disciples and to baptize. Sure one can use politics to make disciples, but politics is simply a vehicle to making disciples (as any job can be). It's not a vehicle of "control" as many politicized Christians are trying to leverage politics. When I've asked many Christ followers why politics is so important to them, their answers boil down to control, not making disciples. They say, "We've lost our way. We need to be a Christian nation again!" or "We need to gain back the moral high ground!" These answers expose the reality that *we've lost our way.* First of all, we've *never* been a "Christian nation." The men who founded our country were Free Masons, which is a very dangerous cult. It becomes more about making people do what we want them to do (or not do) than caring for people's hearts as Jesus did.

---

41   Shane Claiborne, *Jesus for President* (Grand Rapids: Zondervan, 2008), 235.

We know we are the growing minority and dislike losing our place in the front of the line. Many Christians are having a hard time no longer being the "top dog" and thus lash out in this frustration. Here's something we need to remember: the church isn't supposed to be the top dog in culture. We grow better and healthier followers when we are *not*—just look at history!

Second of all, we see no outer enforcement by the early church to make people moral, especially not in the political realm. The people, primarily the Pharisees, who focused on the outward appearances, were verbally told off by Jesus for their behavior; *Jesus and the early church show us that living out our faith is the most effective way to real-life change for us and others.* To force someone to do things "our way" only embitters them to the person we claim to follow and whom we hope they too follow one day. As followers of Christ we must come to understand this core truth of the Christian life: living out the gospel to model it is far more important than trying to force others to "be like us." When we live out the gospel, we win people's *hearts*, not just their approval or their behavior. The reality is that those who do not follow Christ can't do what the Bible says anyway because they do not have the power of the Spirit to urge and help them to do so (as we delved into in a previous chapter).

This is what makes Jesus good—He cares more about our heart than our behavior. Jesus would not run for President because He desires to be our Prophet, Priest, and King. Once we understand Him to be the Prophet and Priest, Him being King becomes much easier. *Knowing He loves us and has our best in mind makes it so much easier to trust and obey His will.* It becomes more of a second nature than like obedience. We begin to do as He has commanded automatically because His Spirit within us gives us the power to do so. We are charged to display the restored life now, to model and live out our allegiance to the better King now. Which means *we live on this earth the way He did*: living and dying, loving and guiding—not yelling and screaming, backbiting, and idolizing our patriotism.

My opinion on politics *in* church is that it is a destroyer of community and unity within the body. If we are believers in Christ, and are made new by the Spirit, it doesn't matter what your political background or party is.

In my heart, I truly believe we as the Body of Christ need to remain united more than ever in this tumultuous time. I fear our political party has become more of a god to us than God Himself, patriotism has covered over our vigor for the church, and our campaigns for our candidates have overshadowed our evangelism for Christ. Sure we have a duty to lead this country for Jesus and desire the most "Christ-like" candidate to take the Presidency, but we must stop fooling ourselves. Christ does not reign in the hearts of many in office. The nation we desire to have will never happen until Christ returns. God will bless this nation through us, His church, as we serve this world through our love of one another and the lost, and we've been lacking hoping our candidate and the country will do what we are supposed to do.

JESUS CALLS US TO HONOR THE KING, NOT BASH HIM

Be subject for the Lord's sake to every human institution, whether it be to the emperor as supreme, or to governors as sent by him to punish those who do evil and to praise those who do good. For this is the will of God, that by doing good you should put to silence the ignorance of foolish people. Live as people who are free, not using your freedom as a cover-up for evil, but living as servants of God. Honor everyone. Love the brotherhood. Fear God. Honor the emperor (1 Peter 2:13-17).

Lastly, I believe that we are not to bash those in leadership of our country. Whether the person in office is who you voted for or not, falling into the American, freedom of speech trap of being "able" to say whatever we want and defaming, demeaning, and degrading our leader publicly is wrong. When a non-believer sees Christians bashing our political leaders, it serves only to prove non-believers right—Christians are no different, or worse, than themselves.

If any group had any right to go on a tirade against their authorities, it was the early church. Nero was burning them as entertainment; they were hunted, hated, murdered, forced into hiding, and otherwise outlaws. Yet, in the book of Acts, we see no verbal retaliation on the church's part. They did not go into the public square and defame Nero. They did not begin a political revolt. They did not stage a coup. They humbly submitted. Peter goes on record to make sure the church maintained this stance. Here, we see Peter encouraging the church to respect authority and to *honor* the emperor! This, to me, is absolutely mind blowing. In fact, it wasn't until I heard a sermon on this subject back in my early twenties that I began to apply this message to my life. The preacher, an extremely wise Bible professor, opened up this passage and demanded that we live like we were commanded to and honor our president, no matter who that person may be. It literally changed my whole perspective on how I engage the political world and how I can honor the "emperor." I bet we will see a tide turn if we choose to live out this idea.

Again, if we could divorce some of our rhetoric from the political sphere, I think we could do a much better job of showing how Jesus is good. The question we really need to wrestle with is, "Can our faith honestly be divorced from our political life?" I think in many respects there are places where it should be, but CAN it? Issues like the sanctity of life, sanctity of marriage, taking care of the poor, war, the death penalty, and gun control are all considered "faith issues" by many Christians. Most of our "hot button" items we back up with the justification of our faith and say these are our "moral standards based off of my interpretation of my beliefs." So we make the political party that backs our interpretations with supreme religious gusto.

I am not saying backing these issues with our faith is wrong. They are all *important* topics to consider. However, the problem comes when our "moralistic" agenda is more important than the candidate who we are backing, simply because he aligns with our agenda. This happened in the last election, and many Christians didn't even bat an eye at this hypocrisy. The candidate was not a Christian and was in fact part of a religious cult, but espoused "Christian morals" so many backed him without any qualms. That is a serious failure to judge correctly.

In my opinion, we seem to be hanging our hats way too much on the agenda of moralism and our agendas, letting go of things that would have frustrated us even just four years ago. I think my biggest frustration in this is with our famous Christian leaders who back a candidate because they have a mutually beneficial relationship, not because they sought the Holy Spirit. For example, if a famous Christian with a large platform backs a candidate, you can bet that someone from the party of that candidate will give more money that year to that Christian's ministry. The arrangement is mutually beneficial. Many of you reading this may not believe this happens, but I assure you that it does.

How can we begin to refuse to allow our politics to interfere so deeply with our faith? We must begin to pray, seek, and ask hard questions. We need to ensure that the way we go about politics is Spirit led, not man led. We must look to the example of Jesus and see how very little He discussed the politics of His day and instead lived out His politics. We don't do this very much. Many who publicly talk about "helping the poor" but do not even lift a finger to help out are hypocrites.

Jesus is good in the midst of politics because He lived out His belief. He didn't force His belief on anyone but simply drew them in by His love. Jesus asks us to live out our beliefs as well. We can put action to our ideals. For example, if you feel the need to cut welfare, find ways to help the poor who will be affected. If you are pro-life, help with organizations that help push for that agenda practically or find ways to support teen moms. We can have political ideals, but we can act upon them rather than shout about them.

When we look at the life of Jesus and study His life and His words, rarely do we see Him interacting with the world of politics. In one of the places where He does interact, He doesn't defame or deplete the government He is under; He does the opposite in fact! My prayer is that we, the Bride of Christ, can model that Jesus is good, because **He is good.**

REFLECTIONS ON "JESUS WOULD NOT RUN FOR PRESIDENT"

1. What's one thing you can apply to your life from this chapter?

2. What's one thing that's hard to accept in this chapter?.

3. What's at least one thing you can agree with or take away from this chapter?

4. What are the things that you don't agree with? Why?

JESUS DESIGNED ALL FORMS OF LOVE

WHEN I WAS IN FIRST or second grade, I thought I was in love. There was this young lady in my school named Meghan Diner, and I felt like she was the *one*. I went on a search to find ways to express love to girls (especially Meghan) and share the deep feelings I was experiencing. My young mind went to TV and the radio, and I soon found my muse. My parents had recently watched a movie *The Body Guard;* it was a big deal and had just come out on VHS, so everyone was talking about the film. The song *I Will Always Love You* by Whitney Houston was featured in the film, and was all over the radio too. So I knew this was what I needed to bring to the table: a song. But not just any song. I needed to sing *the* song—*this* song. One day during recess, I got in trouble and was put on the wall. I felt this moment of stardom was what I needed. From the wall of bad kids, I proceeded to sing loudly to Meghan the song *I Will Always Love You*. I think we "liked" each other for a week and the relationship ended. I didn't know how to love Meghan, so I turned to the world to define it for me. It ended up being a silly story, but a sad reality.

This story shows something important—*the world's definition of love is diluted and lacking.* Great films like *The Body Guard,* and many other chick-flicks, tend to attempt a legendary search in order to define something as powerful as love, and they usually fail pretty badly in their journey and definition. This false expectation of a whimsical, blissful, romanticized version of love is not strong enough to withstand real life. However, there is a real, powerful understanding of love, and it comes from the Holy Scriptures. The Spirit of God breathed these words into the men who wrote them and leads us to understand them.

Love began with God, and He is the designer and creator of love. Love comes from God because God is love.

YOU CAN'T KNOW LOVE IF YOU DON'T KNOW GOD

Anyone who does not love does not know God, because God is love (1 John 4:8).

When we learn about love, we learn about God, and when we learn about God, we learn about love. To many, I am aware that this seems arrogant and religiously manipulative. However, when one looks at the love the world offers, it leaves one cold, doesn't it? Love that is defined by emotionally romanticized affection will end, yet the current culture at large pedals the love that brings death everywhere.

Many people walk from relationship to relationship, seeking this emotionally romanticized love and believing they've found it—only to be let down and depressed by the sad reality of false love. When one looks at the narrative of God, one sees a love that is unlike any other love in history. One can view a picture of a love that has lasted for centuries. The narrative of God is quite literally a story of love.

Even the love of philosophy can leave one wanting more. The love of philosophy comes closer to the reality of what love is, but still doesn't go deep enough. God defines for us what love is and takes deep care in choosing the words in which He describes it for us. His definition doesn't simply encompass one aspect of love either. It encompasses the *three main areas* of the soul's need for love—*phileo* (friendship love); *agape* (an unwavering, unconditional commitment to the ultimate well-being of the other); and *eros* (sexual or romantic love, which we will discuss in the next chapter). In His Word, He clearly explains what these aspects of love are and are not.

When Paul wrote his letter to the Corinthians, he paused with a powerful poem on what unconditionally, sold out, never-leaving love would look like. The first thing he states is that *true love puts up with the mess of real life.*

TRUE LOVE PUTS UP WITH THE MESS OF REAL LIFE

Love is patient and kind; love does not envy or boast; it is not arrogant or rude. It does not insist on its own way; it is not irritable or resentful; it does not rejoice at wrongdoing, but rejoices with the truth. Love bears all things, believes all things, hopes all things, endures all things (1 Cor. 13:4-7).

Here, in this portion of the Scripture, we see that *agape* love is patient. Our English word simply doesn't do justice to the real meaning. The word Paul used literally means: "Love is long-suffering." The definition of long-suffering is: "having or showing patience in spite of troubles, especially those caused by other people."[42] This means: *agape* love deals with the mess of life. Real love doesn't run when troubles come, even if the person we are "loving" causes these troubles. In our culture, this mindset is counter to the normal belief. Once someone or something causes problems, we are taught to throw it away and get a new one. Suffering is bad, and if a person causes you to suffer, culture tells you that person doesn't love you—because *love* is always supposed to *feel* nice, like kittens and rainbows. My friends, real love puts up with the mess of real life and means *choosing* to walk in the mess with the people you love, not run from them, or their mess. You can't love Cheetos like this! We, in our culture, have so dulled the word love that it is quite overused and almost meaningless, but love is incredible and was always meant to be so. God doesn't just preach at us to love this way and ignore His own advice. No, God practices what He preaches. Take a look at a quick view into the story of Hosea.

When the LORD first spoke through Hosea, the LORD said to Hosea, "Go, take to yourself a wife of whoredom and have children of whoredom, for the land commits great whoredom by forsaking the LORD (Hosea 1:2).

---

42   https://www.google.com/#q=define+long-suffering

And the LORD said to me, "Go again, love a woman who is loved by another man and is an adulteress, even as the LORD loves the children of Israel, though they turn to other gods and love cakes of raisins." So I bought her for fifteen shekels of silver and a homer and a lethech of barley. And I said to her, "You must dwell as mine for many days. You shall not play the whore, or belong to another man; so will I also be to you." For the children of Israel shall dwell many days without king or prince, without sacrifice or pillar, without ephod or household gods. Afterward the children of Israel shall return and seek the LORD their God, and David their king, and they shall come in fear to the LORD and to His goodness in the latter days (Hosea 3:1-5).

Here, we see God not only giving us a living picture of His long-suffering with Israel, but we also see Him promising to keep loving His people that way. I am Gomer, yet God still redeemed me while I was whoring myself out to the Devil. How do I know the definition of love from God is true? I know because I've experienced it. He has bought me with His blood, and I'm washed clean, just as Hosea bought back his wife from the pimp! It's that deep and rich, my friends. He's also done it for you. When we are filled with Him, we too can love like this, and when those we love are filled with Him, they can love us like this too. Love is long-suffering, but it is also sacrificial and serving. True love isn't about itself.

TRUE LOVE LIVES FOR OTHERS, NOT ITSELF (1 COR. 13:5-8A)

True love does not insist on its own way. If a guy or a gal tells you that in order to prove your love, you must or should have sex, this person has simply proven to you that *he or she doesn't really love you.* Love can't wait to give, but lust can't wait to get. Love, when done right in a relationship, is fulfilling, because each person is seeking to serve the other. When each person is looking to pour out everything to the other, you have a healthy relationship of true love. False love happens when one party seeks his or her own way and desires the significant other to seek to please him or her as well. Love lives to serve; it does not seek to be served. Nor does it keep records of wrongdoing.

Love, designed by God, is the most incredible reality of life. *Agape* means unconditional and unending. In fact, Paul states in 1 Corinthians 13:8a that love never ends. It never settles for less, and it never quits. In the deep understanding of love, there is no falling in and out of it. You are simply loving or not loving. We have so cheapened the idea of love that we believe it can end, but it endures all things. *Love endures all things; it doesn't mean that love affirms all things.* Love can come in the form of affirmation, but affirmation of everything the person does or is doing is not necessary for love to be given. If I believe it is wrong for you to do it, I don't affirm a certain action. Yet, because I love you, even if you choose that action, I will still be here for you and with you. I probably will never affirm the thing you're doing as right, but I will never leave you. This is the love that God gives, yet many times the evangelical world misses it.

We see this love in the continuing story of God's narrative. God never gave up on me, and He will never give up on you either. He practices what He preaches. He is always patient, always kind, and always enduring and bearing all things. We too can experience this unconditional love here on earth.

God desires not only that we love the way He calls us to love, but also that we experience the love He has designed. When we fall for the false love our culture has designed, it breaks God's heart because He has designed us for better. He has given us this beautiful poetic description to show us not only how to love, but how He has designed us to be loved. When we look deeper into the Scriptures to see what love is, we also see that *love knows*. We just discussed what *agape* looks like and it is deep and rich. There are three aspects of love as we mentioned, not just one. The love that *knows* is the aspect of love known as *phileo*. Some have called it the love of companionship or friendship.

In England, long ago, some men met weekly in a restaurant called The Eagle and the Child. These men wrestled with deep issues of spirituality, life, love, and bringing forth ideas for books, both fiction and non-fiction. This group of friends or band of brothers was known as the Inklings. Two famous members were J.R.R. Tolkien and C.S. Lewis. These two men grew close, became best friends, and helped encourage one another to write and publish their books of fantastical fiction. They had a now-famous friendship that was rooted in the love of companionship. C.S. Lewis, in his book *The Four Loves,* talks about this friendship love as one of utmost importance in one's life. Here's how he describes the genesis of this type of love: "Friendship arises out of mere companionship when two or more of the companions discover that they have in common some insight or interest or even taste which the others do not share and which, till that moment, each believed to be his own unique treasure (or burden)."[43] When people in general begin to see they are not alone and there are people who get them, they slowly begin to reveal more of themselves and develop a deep, rich friendship. This type of love is also described in the Scriptures. In Hebrew, the word is *rayah,* and in the Greek, the word is *phileo* or *philadelphia.* Lewis (and I believe Scripture agrees) would go on to say that this form of *phileo* love is vitally important in a person's life. Too often, we take only the emotional and romantic aspect of *phileo* and miss the deeper reality of this type of love. This love offers deep companionship rooted in authenticity.

Lewis saw the importance of a life balanced with *phileo.* Emotions are an important aspect to love, but are not the only driving force. Although *phileo/rayah* is expressed as emotional and, sometimes, romantic love, it is also the love of companionship. Many times, we miss this. *We over simplify love by defining it only as an emotional reality.* Yet, here we come to a definition of the second aspect of love, which could be defined as "a decision of companionship, where one is seeking to know and be known." There may be attraction, but in *phileo* there

---

43   C.S. Lewis, *The Four Loves* (San Diego: Harcourt Books, 1960) 65.

doesn't always have to be. It is intrinsic in a romantic relationship but is not just for romance.

We live in a world, both in and out of the church, that fails to rightly define and explain what love truly is. *The current definition of love is shallow and lives only on the surface.* There is more to love than simply emotions, there is unwavering commitment as we discussed earlier, as well as a deep, side-by-side decision of companionship.

WE WERE MADE FOR DEEP, RICH, AND AUTHENTIC COMPANIONSHIP

And the man and his wife were both naked and were not ashamed (Gen. 2:25).

One of the most beautiful passages on not only our connection to one another, but also to God Himself, is this passage in Genesis. It defines the utter reality of the core of the *phileo* type of love. There is a sense of open honesty, a sense of living an open life with those we choose to love in this manner. We discussed earlier about *agape/ ahava* love, which is defined as an unwavering commitment. Here, the focus changes and that is why it is a separate type of love from *agape.*

Imagine a three-legged stool. It clearly needs all three legs in order to be functional and be fully used as it was designed to do, which is to hold weight. Each leg on this stool represents one of the three aspects of love we've been discussing. All are powerful and necessary in their own right, but it is when all three are combined that you find the full reality of the love that God has designed for us to experience in a deep, marital relationship. Take one of these legs out, and you are left with a useless hunk of ugly-looking wood. This is why the three aspects of love are so important to understand. They are needed for a healthy marriage and should begin to be discovered through dating, or courting if you prefer. I am simply taking the stool of your relational life and putting legs on it.

One of the deep realities of the soul is that our souls desire to know and be known. We have a deep, intrinsic desire for deep companionship to the level of being naked and unashamed. We are wired with this desire to really be known and understood. Yet, we struggle to find any friendship, dating or otherwise, where we don't experience ourselves being forced to wear masks. We fear that if we are truly known, the person will walk away and never end up giving us the fullness of love we are longing for. Knowing "facts" about someone is not really *knowing* them. You could know all there is to know about someone on Facebook, as far as raw data goes, and still never have met them face-to-face. Phileo is the love of *knowing*. We experience this deep revealing of self and see others who love us this way by showing themselves to us. We are knowing them and being known by them. This is true friendship—true companionship.

Love in all its forms is a choice. We choose to love; it is not a fleeting reality. *We don't choose our families, but we do choose our friends.* Once you decide to go all in with *agape* love, it becomes second nature, the person becomes in some sense a part of you, and the choice of commitment was settled long ago. Here, with this expression of love, there is a consistent choice; there is a daily choice of walking in companionship and revealing self. Many people verbally applaud community, but this is where most community's break down—they simply don't want to be this honest. Although there is a desire to be known, there is a deep fear of being rejected as well that usually wins the battle.

Attraction draws us to this point and that is why this love is where most relationships, dating and non-dating begin, yet to remain in *phileo* there is a conscience, daily choice. As friendships grow and deepen, so does *phileo*. In Genesis 2:25, this type of intimacy was the original intent of God for His people; there was no shame at being naked with one another and with God. There are certain people we let in. We may say we "love" people, but we are usually using the cultural understanding, not this deeper, Biblical understanding. *Are you safe to be yourself around the people you "love"?* This type of love is a love that expresses itself in companionship and is honest about its fears, doubts, struggles, and joys.

This passage in Genesis lets us know that we were created for a *phileo* community. We were designed for the intrinsic desire to live naked and unashamed with God and with others, most closely obviously with our spouse, but also with people of our own gender. Men, we need men we can experience *phileo* with; women, you need women you can experience *phileo* with as well. We are created to live in community, not isolation. *Phileo* love was designed for marital relationships, but it is also the love we need outside of that type of relationship.

LOVE CAN MAKE FRIENDSHIPS CLOSER THAN FAMILY

A friend loves at all times, and a brother is born for adversity (Prov. 17:17).

A man of many companions may come to ruin, but there is a friend who sticks closer than a brother (Prov. 18:24).

These passages in Proverbs discuss the close-knit relationship of the type of love we are discussing. A friend loves at all times and there is a friend who sticks closer than a brother. We've heard these truths before, but have we really experienced them? Have we seen friends stick closer than family? Have we experienced friends who are willing to see us as we are and still hang around? Or are the majority (or all) of our friendships shallow? We have a deep desire to know and be known built within us and are not meant to live in isolation. These types of relationships are possible. True community starts with us being willing to be a friend who loves at all times and allows others to be vulnerable and open.

Jesus was such a friend to His disciples and a man named Lazarus. When His friend Lazarus died, Jesus wept and those gathered there exclaimed, "You see how He loved (*phileo*) him!?" (John 11:36). The book of John records many instances of using the word *phileo*, mainly by

John describing himself as "the disciple who Jesus loved." John knew Jesus knew him and stayed. Jesus knew everything about John and yet still loved him as His own family.

The main angle I am coming at with the idea of *phileo* type love is that of two lovers finding this type of love within their relationship, because as we will see in the next chapter, all three aspects of love are absolutely necessary to develop a real, long and lasting marriage between two people. Many times in today's dating world, this type of love, the kind where we can be ourselves, is always desired but rarely realized. Even people who've been married for decades fail to live out this aspect of love, yet it is vital to a healthy relationship. This is not just for dating/engagement/marriage-type relationships either. We were created to experience this type of love with others as well; this is the love of true friendship. May we seek to be people who love those who are seeking to be known by us, and may we be people who allow others we love to truly know us.

Jesus is good because He designed all forms of love. He not only designed them, but also gave us a map to understanding them. Love can be dangerous, wild and scary at times, but if we lean into *real* love, the kind that Jesus designed, it can be life-giving and safe. Why do we settle for aspects of love that do not truly satisfy? I think because deep down, we are afraid of rejection. We fear truly being known as *phileo* love requires because we don't love ourselves, so how could someone else?

The reality is this: Jesus knows you and still loves you. I know this causes my heart to doubt: how can something be that good? Then I reflect on my experience with this deep love He has for me and *know* it to be true. Jesus is good because He loves this way. There truly is no better love than His.

REFLECTIONS ON "JESUS DESIGNED ALL FORMS OF LOVE"

1. What are your thoughts on the three aspects of love mentioned?

2. How have you seen these aspects of love surface in your life personally?

3. Why do you think this approach is or isn't best?

4. How can you allow Christ's design for love to change the way in which you live?

JESUS DESIGNED SEX AND MARRIAGE

THIS LOVE OF KNOWING, *PHILEO,* flows us into the next aspect of love—the sexual expression of love—which in the Greek is *eros.* Jesus is good because He designed love, which includes the design for this expression of love. Sex is an awkward topic, I know. I remember when I was a fifth grader and was introduced to sex in school. Graphs, charts, and cartoonish imagery were my introduction into the realm of "sexual understanding." All the dudes in the room had to keep cracking jokes just so we could get over the uncomfortable nature of the topic. Next, as a freshman in an inner-city public school, I remember the weird shyness that came over me as we were shown how to put condoms on bananas and were told all about sex from a simply physical understanding.

Let us let down our guard a bit as we discuss this topic. Get comfortable because as we unfold the issues of sex and a little bit about sexuality, I think we will discover that God's design for sex is awesome and something we all will desire to experience. After all, we were all designed to enjoy sex. I think the reason it's uncomfortable is because the *culture has "pornified" sex, while the church has sometimes demonized it.* Sex is an important topic for us all, in particular for you as a millennial. The stats on this hookup culture are staggering. One study reveals that 77.7% of college females admitted to "hooking up." This means that these young women have one-night stands with young men they either don't know at all or barely know for the sole purpose of physical gratification. For males, the percentage is even higher—84.2%.[44] There is clearly a belief that sex is simply physical. I'm here to

---

44   Matt Chandler, *The Mingling of Souls: God's Design for Love, Marriage, Sex and Redemption* (Colorado Springs: David C. Cook, 2015), 52.

tell you that sex has not one aspect, but three. Many people, from all generations, have believed the lie that sex is simply physical and have paid drastically for the belief in a lie.

Sex has been glorified for the physical pleasure it can bring, but it is not simply a physical act; sex is spiritual and emotional as well. When we leave out the other two aspects of sexuality, we lose the full design of sex, like missing the best-tasting wine and instead trade it in for a cheaper taste. This is why the woman, who some believe is the lover of Solomon, in Song of Solomon states, "I adjure you, O daughters of Jerusalem, by the gazelles or the does of the field, that you not stir up or awaken love until it pleases" (2:7). Solomon's lover desires to warn the daughter's of Jerusalem, as well as all of us, to be cautious with the fullness of love, which culminates with sex. Too often, we cheapen sex because the culture around us no longer shares the fullness of what sex is to be. God designed sex to be so much more.

SEX IS DESIGNED TO BE A SPIRITUAL ACT

When the LORD first spoke through Hosea, the LORD said to Hosea, "Go, take to yourself a wife of whoredom and have children of whoredom, for the land commits great whoredom by forsaking the LORD" (Hosea 1:2).

Sex is not merely physical; we know this because when one is sexually violated it leaves deep scars, not just on one's body, but on victims' emotions and very souls. Sexual violation is the hardest thing to overcome emotionally and, for many, spiritually. If sex were just a physical act, long-lasting wounds wouldn't be connected to it. I know we can all agree on that issue, so then we must seek to see how the soul, the emotions, and the body are connected to this one act—that's how sex is designed to work best. Just as in any designed creation, there are certain conditions in which that creation works the best. Think of a laptop computer. It needs to stay dry and at a certain temperature. It needs a proper power supply and maintenance in order to remain fully functional. No one complains about these parameters. We simply do them because we want the best from our computers. We, being created beings, have certain parameters with which we need to follow in order to be the best us as well. God, our designer, also designed sex, and after creation God said, "It is Good!" He made sex—so we know it shouldn't be demonized. Since He designed sex, we should pay attention to what He says about it.

God designed sex to be spiritual. In Exodus 20:3 and 14 we see two of the Ten Commandments: "You shall have no other gods before me" and "You shall not commit adultery." In the story of Hosea, we see both of these commandments being violated, but God asked Hosea to have Gomer as a wife as an image of how Israel was being unfaithful to God, but He loved them anyway. Here we see a declaration that when we bow to other gods, we are whoring ourselves out and violating a covenant. The first commandment is essentially saying that this covenant won't work with other lovers in the mix. Throughout the Scripture, God uses the imagery of marriage to define the reality of love being exclusive. Specifically, *sexual love is the physical representation of the spiritual condition of one's exclusiveness.* The ancient Hebrews understood the spirituality of sex. The above commandments were given by God and received by Moses under the "cloud of God's glory." Vows were made under the tent of God. In the ancient Jewish culture, and still today, the wedding vows are done under the *chuppa*, which is a canopy representing the glory and presence of God. The wedding, however, is not complete when the vows are done. In ancient times, the couple would leave and the crowd would follow and the *chuppa* would be carried above the couple, following them to their bed, where the *chuppa* was set up above the bed to represent the presence of God in their sex lives. They would then have sex under the presence of God (with everyone waiting outside), and after sex they'd go back out to the crowd; only then could the reception start. The presence of God in their marriage, and thus the spiritual nature of the couple's relationship, wasn't complete without sex!

God designed sex in such a way that He would bless it with His presence when done as designed. When sex happens outside of God's design, the presence of God is not in it, thus we immediately lose one third of what sex is designed to be.

SEX IS DESIGNED TO BE AN EMOTIONAL ACT

The watchmen found me as they went about in the city. "Have you seen him whom my soul loves?" (Song 3:3).

> "Therefore a man shall leave his father and his mother and hold fast to his wife, and the two shall become one flesh?" So they are no longer two but one flesh. What therefore God has joined together, let not man separate (Matt. 19:5-6).

The concept of "oneness" is a concept of mystery. When two people have sex, they become one. In the Scriptural understanding, it is "the knitting of two hearts into one." This is clearly indicative of an emotional connection, and one could argue a spiritual connection as well. Sure there is some physical truth to the statement, but why would Jesus then say, "What therefore God has joined together, let not man separate,"[45] if this was just a physical understanding?

The bride in Song of Solomon in 3:3 is searching for the one her "soul loves" and eagerly awaits both the wedding and the consummation of this marriage with an emotional desire. There is a longing to no longer be on her own, but to be one with her husband. She was starting to be deeply emotionally involved. After marriage and sex, her heart was so one with his, and so emotionally invested, that she said of him, "My beloved (*dod*) is radiant and ruddy, distinguished among ten thousand." She loves her husband (now also her sexual lover) so deeply that she can't contain her emotional excitement. She's talking to all the women in Jerusalem. She declares to them that he is incredible.

---

45   Mark 10:9

See her deep emotional investment? It's because sex knits two into one and there is deep emotional connection there, particularly for the woman. Too often men give emotional "love" to get sex, and women give sex to get emotional "love." This sadly breaks down the full impact that sex can have and lessens something designed to be all-captivating.

SEX IS DESIGNED TO BE A PHYSICAL ACT

He brought me to the banqueting house, and his banner over me was love. Sustain me with raisins; refresh me with apples, for I am sick with love (Song 2:4-5).

Your lips drip nectar, my bride; honey and milk are under your tongue; the fragrance of your garments is like the fragrance of Lebanon (Song 4:11).

When understood in its context, Song of Songs is extremely sexually graphic. The two portions above make it clear that sex is supposed to be physical and these are *tame* portions. Every aspect of *dod* (Hebrew form of *eros*) in Song of Solomon before chapter 4 were contextualized and explained through Hebrew as an aspect of sexual longing. Everything after chapter 4 is sexually explicit, detailing in many ways how these lovers make love. If God didn't want us to physically enjoy sex, this portion of Scripture wouldn't be here, nor would our bodies be able to enjoy it.

If sex was designed for procreation only, why would God place receptors in certain areas of our body? The answer is, He wouldn't. God intended sex to be physically pleasurable! Also, it's important to note, that desiring to have sex with the man or woman you love before marriage isn't wrong either. Note the comment about the raisins. Raisins in this culture were a symbol of sex; they were expensive, rare, rich, and desired. Solomon's lover is explaining that when they're married, she'll be ready for the raisins, because she is sick with love. The word "love" as the banner however is *ahavah*, or *agape*, saying because

Solomon loves me this way, I'm ready. He is deeply committed to me as *his,* so I am ready and wanting to give my body to him. This is the way sex was designed, to be desired when the full reality of love was delivered and a marriage was done. *Think again of love as a three-legged stool.* Now imagine two legs of the stool are ripped off. When we simply try and use sex only as the culture tries to allure us to do, we have a weak stool. Eventually it will fail. Think too of a flame. Each aspect of love is a flame from a lighter, but when combined they make a roaring fire! We've been trained to seek all the heat of love in the one flame of *eros,* rather than the bonfire it was meant to be, through the other aspects of love.

Sometimes, however, within the church we decry all sexual desire and end up shutting people down sexually. This happens to such a degree that after getting married, many Christians still feel that sex is dirty and wrong. Healthy sexuality is a beautiful and wonderful thing, but only in the right timing. Remember the bride's warning: *do not arouse love until it pleases.* She's stating a God-breathed reality that sex outside of the right timing (within marriage and when the three flames of love are combined) will be detrimental.

The statement I made early on about how culture pornifies and the church sometimes demonizes sex is true. Sex is meant to be in the context of marriage; it is not just an animal-like act of physical desire. Nor is it an ugly thing we shouldn't long for or desire. Sex is what we do with the desire. God in His Word tells us to be drunk on sex within the context of marriage, to live in it, and allow the three flames of love to ignite our lives until we are drunk within it! Yet we can't grasp the totality of what sex is meant to be outside of marriage; we get only small heat from something meant to be added to a bonfire. Maybe some people reading this have fallen sexually. Does this mean you've screwed it up and there's no hope? Absolutely not! There is redemption from all sin (1 John 1:9)! We can be purified from *anything,* and God can reset our lives on a path towards the bonfire of love He has for us. There may need to be healing, and He will heal as well! God desires our best. He desires we experience the fullness of the love He's designed—*agape, phileo,* and *eros!*

The amazing thing about the Scripture is that it doesn't simply tell us what we need to do, it also continuously gives us the "how" as well. The book of Song of Solomon is no different in this. We've seen the three aspects of love and the need for developing a three-legged stool in our love lives, but how is this done? Earlier, I stated that in the first three chapters in Song of Solomon the word *dod,* or in Greek *eros,* was used for a sense of sexual longing. In the rest of this chapter we see the basis for how to develop a beautiful dance that will culminate in the fulfillment of the sexual longing—the final leg to the stool.

I am not a dancer by any stretch of the imagination. The times I come close to actually dancing are when I dance with my beautiful little girl or slow dance in the kitchen with my darling bride. Despite my lack of dancing ability, I do know that dance is more measured than natural. What I mean by that is in dance there are specific steps and certain ways in which the leader leads in order to make the dance appear flawless. To dance well, there must be an intentional following of the steps and certain rules. Dating is the same. Dating can be terrible, or it can be wonderful. Dating can lead to a beautiful dance, or an awful one. I believe this portion of the Scripture gives us a picture of a couple in great detail to show us what the beautiful dance would look like, so we too can know how to develop a beautiful dance.

Too often, when it comes to dating, we succumb to a lousy dance. We fumble around trying to get it right time and time again. By this time in our lives we are ready to start seeing the beautiful dance unfold, rather than the dance that brings pain, agony, and frustration to our lives. Together, as we end this chapter on the goodness of Jesus in love and sex, we will seek to answer the question: *How do we experience the beautiful dance?* God has designed many of our hearts in such a way as to crave this dance. We are all hardwired to seek intimacy, and *our heart's desire the intimacy that leads to a great marriage. We sadly have few places to look.* So, let's see through Solomon and his lover how we can have a beautiful dance.

Take a moment and open your Bible to Song of Solomon and read chapters one and two.

Here, we see a budding romance. This young lady and King Solomon have begun their relationship. They saw each other and were interested in beginning a relationship. This acquaintanceship developed into a friendship and then an exclusive relationship. Once they decided they had an attraction towards one another, they began a series of dances that led to the Beautiful Dance of their marriage. Let's learn from their love and the dances they took in order to get to the Beautiful Dance. Matt Chandler, author of *Mingling Souls* of which much of this content stems from, states: "As you pursue a relationship into the world of dating, don't simply look for someone who reciprocates your attraction but one who reciprocates your desire to honor Jesus in your relationship above all else."[46] This I believe is the first thing we must seek to find directly after we find ourselves attracted or allured to someone. Without a reciprocal desire to honor Jesus, these dances we will go into will not work or may be taken out of order, both of which are dangerous for the heart. The first dance step we come in contact with in the lives of this couple is the dance of delight. They truly delight in one another.

THE DANCE OF DELIGHT

Tell me, you whom my soul loves, where you pasture your flock, where you make it lie down at noon; for why should I be like one who veils herself beside the flocks of your companions? If you do not know, O most beautiful among women, follow in the tracks of the flock, and pasture your young goats beside the shepherds' tents (Song 1:7-8).

---

46   Matt Chandler, *The Mingling of Souls: God's Design for Love, Marriage, Sex and Redemption* (Colorado Springs: David C. Cook, 2015), 54.

Here, we see the woman's desire to know where Solomon is going to be. She's no longer just physically attracted to him. She's not asking this question just so she can watch him, but so she can spend time with him. She's beginning to delight in his presence, and she had a desire to develop the delight of knowing, or to deepen the *phileo* love they've been coming to experience. *She saw that Solomon was a man of good character and of good reputation.* She ran it by her friends, and in 1:4b, they let her know her pursuit of Solomon was a good thing. Let's pause here for a moment and rest in this idea. She entrusted her feelings for Solomon to friends she knew she could trust. She knew they would tell her the truth—whether she wanted to hear it or not. She may declare her desire to delight in knowing Solomon, and her friends could have said, "Stay away!" If you've surrounded yourself with good, strong, godly friends, trust their judgment! If as one, they all say, "This person is bad," you'd probably need to heed their warning. *Too often, at this important stage, we ignore all of the wise counsel among us and seek out unwise counsel from "friends" who will tickle our ears with what we want to hear.* We come looking for an echo instead of insight.

My wife Hilary had amazing friends in college. They protected her from bad men and even caused me to prove myself to them as well as to her. I had broken Hilary's heart before, twice actually, so naturally they were skeptical of my desire to be with her again. They basically told Hilary she wasn't allowed to date me until I proved to them that I was serious and wasn't going to break her heart again. As a man, this made me both angry and determined. Hilary, to her credit, listened to her friends. Even though I was irresistible (ha, yeah right), she resisted me because of her friends' warnings and her own timidity of getting hurt again. I implore anyone reading this to take serious stock of what your good, close, Christian friends say about a person you desire to date. Don't simply try and find someone who will echo your desire, look for insight.

The woman's friends approved of Solomon, so she had no fear moving to the next level of delight with him. She then wanted to be where he was, not in the creepy, stalker way, but in a sense of delighting in what he does and where he goes. She longed to know him better and she longed for him to know her better as well. In essence, she is saying, *"I trust you; my friends trust you. Where will you be, so I can follow you there?"* She wanted to be with his friends, know his life, and experience his work so she could know him more and delight deeper in him. This is the moment where a couple goes from "talking" and adds the dating label. The couple has gotten to know each other. It seems there is mutual emotional feelings and attraction. Will they switch their Facebook status or not? Here, she was declaring she wanted to be where he was, so his friends and those around him knew she's his girl and he's her guy. Solomon's response may seem weird, but is actually flirtatious and highly romantic. He's encouraging her to find him. He did not blow off her question with an *"Oh, I'll text you later about that,"* avoiding the topic. He doesn't do the awkward, *"Slow down babe, I thought what we had was good,"* line, but instead he encourages her desire and gave her a trail to follow—a trail that will lead directly to himself. He too desired to grow in his delight of her. He too desired to spend more time with her. The dance of delight is a great place to begin to get to the beautiful dance. Both dancers are assured that this dance is about being delighted in for simply being who they are, not for how beautiful their bodies may or may not be.

Once the dance of delight is established, the next dance can begin—the dance of security. When one person begins to fall for another, safety is a key factor. Will this person break your heart? Can he or she be trusted? Is this person trustworthy? These questions are big in the steps of the dance of security and ultimately in the beautiful dance.

THE DANCE OF SECURITY

I am very dark, but lovely, O daughters of Jerusalem,
like the tents of Kedar, like the curtains of Solomon. Do
not gaze at me because I am dark, because the sun has
looked upon me. My mother's sons were angry with me;
they made me keeper of the vineyards, but my own vineyard I have not kept! (Song 1:5-6).

In a moment of deep honesty in verses 5-6, the woman in the
story reveals one of her deepest insecurities. She is insecure about
her looks and her background. She is a Shulamite woman who grew
up on a vineyard and the sun has made her skin dark. She grew up
outside working while most women pursuing a king have not. Due
to her exposure to the sun, her skin is darker than most women.
These two issues in her heart act as deep insecurities. She is essentially asking, "How could you love a dark woman from such a
background as I?"

She is beginning the process of exposing her inner self to Solomon.
She is seeking to be known, even if it's scary. Even if exposing her
fears backfires, she loves him enough to be honest. Will her honesty
be reciprocated? Will her openness backfire? She has to try. You see,
even before anything physical happens here, this couple is showing
us the proper way to dance. It's as if they are saying, "If I can't trust
you with my heart, there is no way I can trust you with my body." Too
often, we switch that around and try to test the waters with our bodies.
Yet as we saw earlier, sex is not just a physical act; it is spiritual and
emotional as well. This part of the dance solidifies the ability to be as
Genesis 2:25 states, "naked and unashamed."

I compare you, my love, to a mare among Pharaoh's chari-
ots. Your cheeks are lovely with ornaments, your neck with
strings of jewels (Song 1:9-10).

Solomon responds with a beautiful composition. He answered her question of "am I good enough" with a comparison to a horse. Now, today this may be an insult, but he was stating that she was one of a kind, beautiful, and he loved her. He dispelled her fears. *A mate who is worth your love will be a one who seeks to dispel your fears, not to exploit them.* He didn't use her openness against her. He didn't ignore her fears, rather he spoke right to them and let her know there should be no fear for he loved her as she was. There was authenticity there and care shown for what was shared. We have been designed with the absolute need to be secure, especially women. Many times, men do not step up to the plate to bring security for the women they profess to love. Too often boys prance around calling themselves men simply so they can get into a girl's pants. Men, we are called to be men who sacrifice self, not push self above all else. Let me now challenge you to be men who bring security, not selfishness.

Once the Dance of Security is in place, the dance of commitment begins to come about as well. As we discussed our souls crave to be known as well as to know. Here we see this couple growing deeply into this place of knowing. Once there is a secure understanding of being known, the heart naturally desires for this to last indefinitely, so it seeks to start the dance of commitment.

THE DANCE OF COMMITMENT (2:4-5; 15 & 16)

He brought me to the banqueting house, and his banner over me was love. Sustain me with raisins; refresh me with apples, for I am sick with love (Song 2:4-5).

Solomon and the woman have already established they are together. They've already begun to open up the depths of their hearts and expose the nakedness of their souls to each other. Now they begin to move into the *agape* zone of love. She states in 2:5b, "His banner over me is **agape**." He has proven his love to her, he has delighted in her, and, despite knowing her darkest fears, and he has loved her anyway. There was a deep commitment there. A banner is a display of ownership in a way, and she's saying, "He owns my heart!" She goes on to say in 2:16a *"My beloved is mine and I am his." She declares that he is the one.* She knew his love was *for* her. She knew she delighted in him, and he in her. She knew that she could be open and honest with him, and he is safe. She declares, *"I'm all in."* The first two dances can take a lot of time before you come to this third dance of commitment. For Hilary and I, the first two dances took 2-3 years—more because of my stupidity as I shared a small portion earlier. These dances needn't be rushed, after all, getting to really know someone takes time. Here in this dance of the relationship, "foxes" (2:15-16) will creep in and test the resolve of the relationship.

Things will try to sneak into your relationship and test your commitment. As the dance unfolds, other portions of your hearts that were previously locked up will now be exposed; a deeper sense of *phileo* comes forth and it will be challenging. This is why there is a call to "catch the little foxes." You will find that even after ten years of marriage, there are still little foxes that come out. Be sure to deal with them as they pop up—don't ignore them.

Here we see that the two loves of *agape* and *phileo* are present. There's also now a longing to connect physically as well (2:4-5). When you discover a partner who is not committed to these two loves and the above dances, run away from that person for he or she is *no good*. There will be mistakes of course along the way, because we humans are not perfect; yet, I implore you as the woman in Song of Solomon does: do not arouse or awaken love until it so desires.

Once these dances are established and the stool is correctly built with both of the first two legs solidly, the next phase of the dance can begin, and this is where the dance becomes beautiful. The foxes are identified, the missteps largely (not completely) corrected, and commitment is secured—beauty can begin.

THE BEAUTIFUL DANCE (SONG OF SOLOMON 5)

The beautiful dance includes God in the midst of it; it's a dance where we are together intoxicated with God and with one another. The friends encourage the couple to be drunk on love! When we combine the three aspects of love, as we've been discussing, the dance that happens will be without comparison in its beauty. Seeking the good of the other while they seek your good is a beautiful thing.

Many people date to get to know other people. I encourage this seeking to be known and to know, but we must be careful and cautious with those we are trying to know and be known by. Are those we are seeking to know loving God? Is their reputation good? Do our friends and family approve? Are they interested more in my *eros* than my *phileo* and *agape*? I implore you not to arouse or awaken love until it so desires. Seek the Lord and your dance will be beautiful.

We see that Jesus is good because He truly has a design for love and sex. When we fully embrace this design, a beautiful dance can happen. When we allow the fullness of love to overwhelm us, first from Him, then from others, we can truly become intoxicated with love. We must remember—God *is* love. So when we are in step with His design, we will be so controlled by His presence that the other things around us will not matter as much as *He* does. We don't have to fall prey to the false loves of this world. We do not have to believe the lies about love and sex that our culture spits at us, for there is a better, more beautiful design. Jesus is *so* good.

REFLECTIONS ON "JESUS DESIGNED SEX AND MARRIAGE"

1. What are your thoughts on the three aspects of sex mentioned?

2. How have you seen these aspects of sex surface in your life personally?

3. Why do you think understanding the fullness of sex is important?

4. How can you seek to not "pornify" or demonize sex?

JESUS LOVES THE LGBTQ COMMUNITY

WHEN ADDRESSING THE ISSUE OF homosexuality, two attitudes are essential: humility and love. In this chapter, I am seeking to approach this topic with humility and love as well as with grace and truth. I think when we come to this topic, there are a lot of emotions that can find their way into it. There are many ideologies that come into play in addition to past pain. Also, for some, a lot of past conversations will come to mind that have happened which have miscommunicated the love and truth of God. I have found when it comes to this particular topic that many people are either on the side of grace, where they don't speak the truth at all about anything, and they're just really gentle and kind and tip-toe around everything. Or they are on the other side of the coin, where they say, "Here's the truth. Deal with it. Suck it up and stop crying like a baby. You're wrong and probably going to hell if you keep thinking this way." We need to be people who live in the *middle*. We need to be people who live in the *grey*.

Too often within our recent religious climate, it has been said to us (or at least suggested) we need to either be on the extreme left or extreme right. But if we're on one of those sides, we automatically hate another group of Christians who we should not be hating but, instead, walking alongside. Many people would argue with me that there isn't hate but sharp disagreement. While I would agree that people can disagree in kindness, as I read through some of the recent Facebook posts and blogs on each side of the issue, hate seems to be more of a viable word to use. There are going to be differences and times we see and talk about certain things differently, and we will most certainly have different political views. However, these differences should never be more important than our discipleship.

As we take this *truth and grace* approach, one thing we need to get straight is: God declares homosexual *conduct* as sinful—not homosexual attraction. You *can in fact* be both gay and Christian, in the midst of sin or not (1 Cor. 6:9-11; James 1:12), just like you can be a fornicator and a Christian or a glutton and a Christian. Rethinking how one views homosexuality will save many Christians from being bigoted against those who are gay and focus the attention on the sin, not the perpetrator of the sin. For too long the evangelical world has focused on the people, missing the real problem in this situation—namely sin.

> Or do you not know that the unrighteous will not inherit the kingdom of God? Do not be deceived: neither the sexually immoral, nor idolaters, nor adulterers, nor men who practice homosexuality, nor thieves, nor the greedy, nor drunkards, nor revilers, nor swindlers will inherit the kingdom of God. And such were some of you. But you were washed, you were sanctified, you were justified in the name of the Lord Jesus Christ and by the Spirit of our God (1 Cor. 6:9-11).

Let me share something with you that I don't think gets talked about when this passage is given. At the very end it says, "And such were some of you." Basically stating: this was your identity. Before Christ, your identity was in the things you found yourself doing. There are people who find their identity in their alcoholism. There are people who find their identity in their sexually immoral living, the way I did when I was in college through looking at porn.

I was studying to be a pastor and struggling with pornography. Maybe many of you are in that same boat of wrestling with sexual immorality. But before you came to Christ that's who you *were*. When we believe in Christ, it's no longer part of our identity; our identity is one that was washed and sanctified by the gospel and love of Jesus Christ. Will you still have those inclinations? Yes. Does that negate your Christianity? No. It does not negate your Christianity because you have these desires, temptations, or sins you find yourself falling into—even if they're addictions. When you say, "I know I'm washed. I know I'm sanctified, but I continue to go towards this, and I almost think it's okay for me," it is your old self, trying to lure you back in. When I was in college, I was a Christian, someone who was going to be a pastor and lead other people to Jesus, and I still wrestled inwardly with looking at pornography. I would convince myself that it was fine and okay, but God kept bringing me back and saying "That's not who you are; that's who you *were.*"

He would say to me, "Will you wrestle with those things? Absolutely. It does not negate your adoption into My kingdom." I believe that this is where we mess up the message of God much of the time. We look at all these people struggling with this list of sins and say, "You're struggling with sexually immorality? You're still a Christian. You're a thief? Eh, aren't we all. You're greedy? You're still a Christian. You're a drunk? Well, you're still a Christian. You revile people? That's okay; we can fix that. You're a swindler? Eh, that's all right. We'll figure that out." However, when someone says they are struggling with being gay, all of the sudden we say, *"I don't know if you're a Christian."* Can I ask why we do that? Do you have any idea why that is the response of many? Do you have any idea why the evangelical world has this as a response? I will give you two things. One is fear. Many Christians who don't have the temptation don't understand it, so to them, it must be demonized. It just doesn't work in their world. They look at that sin and fear it, so rather than deal with it, they demonize the whole issue.

This lack of sympathy saddens my heart because I feel like the church has reacted this way out of fear of the unknown. Many don't understand same-sex attraction, so they vilify it. This happens in human history all the time. If there's something we don't understand, it must be completely off base and rejected.

The second reason Christians react negatively is politics. We allow our politics to change the way we view people, and we allow our politics to change the way we view God. My friends, that's ridiculous. It's asinine to think that my politics are more powerful than the God I serve. So this passage in 1 Corinthians has been abused, misused, and misquoted. It's been one of those things where people are like, "Look! You're *not* going to inherit the kingdom of God! Just get right and stop being gay!" Many Christians have this message and proclaim it loudly without love or humility. The sad reality is that it's only pinpointed towards one person who is struggling with one type of thing—homosexuality. Using the Bible like that is *wrong*. It is an abuse of the Scripture of God. It's sinful and in doing so we become revilers. According to the very passage we say proves someone is messing up, we're actually becoming another person on that list and living in the same type of mess. So we need to come at homosexuality with a completely different view. We need to look at it with hearts full of love, and compassion, seeing ourselves in the story of this mess because we are in with this mess of humanity. And we should not pinpoint certain sins but address the whole person.

Homosexuality is listed alongside other sins. It is not singled out as the worst sin to ever be committed, but often that is how it is treated. Homosexual conduct is just one expression of sin on that list; I am purposefully saying *conduct* and not attraction because it is conduct that is the sin. People within the church often do not make this distinction. Refusing to distinguish between conduct and attraction is a problem for many Christians who may struggle with same-sex attraction and causes the majority of these people to either keep quiet about their struggle or embrace it fully and walk away from the church. In this climate of anti-attraction and conduct, some people within a church might come up to another member and share that they are really struggling with same-sex attraction and think they might be gay. Many times, the reaction may cause evangelical alerts to go off. The church member hearing this confession may think (or worse say): "Oh my goodness! They're sinning! They're in terrible sin! We need to drag this cancer out of them! We need to pray the gay away!"

Sadly, the people who get treated in this manner may begin wondering who they are and try to figure out their identity. Their identity shouldn't even be in question if they know Jesus! And when these struggling Christians get a reaction from another church member, they're like, "Okay. Then I'm just going to go over here, because you hate me. So I'm just going to walk away from the church. I'm done." I've seen this played out in the lives of students at the universities at which I work. As soon as they came to college, they decided to never darken a church door again. These students felt unloved and unwanted by the church.

Jesus would not react this way, because Jesus is good. Jesus would react much differently to their sin (or just temptation) and treat their struggle as any other situation of temptation because temptation is temptation. Imagine if someone were to say: "you know what, I'm really struggling with eating too much." The reaction in the church wouldn't be: "Oh my goodness! We've got to pray the fat out of you! We've got to get this eating disorder under control! We're going to go into your cupboards and take all your Oreos. We've got to take *all* the bad foods! And we've got to take you to this camp for people who struggle with food! At this camp you're going to work out seven days a week!" If the church responded that way, how many people would leave the church?! Why do we respond differently when it comes to the issue of homosexuality? If we believe Jesus is good, we have to ask ourselves that question and be honest with the answer. In today's society, the church has jacked up this conversation. So many people have directed their lives away from Christ and His Bride when they didn't have to. To begin with, attraction nor temptation are sin. Just like when you say you're tempted to look at or do something you shouldn't, no one's going to say you're sinning.

You see the point? And too often when we talk about the gay conversation, we say, "Everything you're struggling with and even your identity as 'gay,' God hates." That's not true. It's one expression of human sin and brokenness, and it's not the worst sin, even though many have declared it to be so. Too often when it comes to sins, we see on the street level of a skyline. Imagine yourself in the city of

Pittsburgh (or any city), and you're on the street level. Can you determine the different heights of each different building? When we look at sin we see all these different heights and say, "Aw, man. That one is worse. Oh man, he's a drunk." That's kind of a "short" sin building. "He's looking at porn." That's a little higher. "That person over there is a glutton." There's very little wrong with that. But that person said they're gay? Oh man, that's the tallest building in this city! On the tallest building of "Sin City" we write *homosexual* up and down that thing and say, "That's the biggest one." But when God sees sin He sees it from a different level. God sees it from above, not street level, and to Him all sin is sin. There is no difference. They may take on different shapes as buildings do, but sin is in fact sin to God.

What about the Scripture that says the sins of the body are worse where Paul lists sexual sins and other sins of the body? When Paul talks about sins of the body being worse, he's not saying they incur a higher wrath from God. He is saying that those sins have emotional ramifications that cause the consequences of those sins to be harder for you to deal with. For example, when you are struggling with gluttony, there's an emotional issue driving that sin. You look in the mirror all the time and you wonder, "What's wrong? What's going on?" If you struggle with anorexia, you look in the mirror and are trying to shape your body into something because you have emotional dissatisfaction. You deal with sex, or a pornographic addiction mixed with masturbation, and there are emotional ramifications, even if it is with a digital woman or a guy. There are ramifications emotionally with all of these sins of the body, so Paul says they are worse for you and harder to deal with and walk through. God didn't say He wanted us to lift up and make these buildings higher; He doesn't want you to freak out and point at anyone dealing with these particular issues. That's not what Paul is saying here at all.

I fear we also respond through a political lens as it pertains to this issue as well. When it comes to the political realm, this is my personal opinion: as I look at the Scriptures and look at the understanding of what Christ calls us to do and not to do, I feel that legislating morality isn't something Christ has called us to. In fact, the gospel spread more when Christianity was not the favorable religion! Members of the early church didn't seek to change the political arena of their day. They largely ignored politics and lived out their faith by the power of the Holy Spirit! We have lost the battle of love seeking to force people into living out our beliefs. Legislating morality? What do I mean? I mean that, for example, we purposefully invaded the political realm to stop gay marriage, which we saw was futile.

Many Christians say to the gay community, "You don't know Jesus, and we don't think you do even if you say you do. However, we're going to force a law upon you that says you can't do what you feel like you should be able to do, because we're going to pass laws against your lifestyle. We're going to make sure, in the legislature of politics, that we force biblical rules upon you." There's one really huge problem with this idea; you and I cannot hold non-Christians to a Christian standard. Here's why: they don't have the Holy Spirit of God living in them. The only way a Christian can even dream to live the Christian life is because of the Holy Spirit (Rom. 8:5-11). If we try to do the Christian life on our own, we might as well walk away. The Scriptures say it's impossible to do on our own. We desperately need the power of the death and resurrection of Jesus living within us in the manifestation of the Spirit of God.

With the idea of legislating morality in mind, let's go back to the idea of gluttony. Gluttony is a sin that is probably mentioned as much, if not more, as homosexuality in the Scriptures. Imagine if we were going to legislate the morality of gluttony, so that we said something like, "Each person can have only a certain amount of caloric intake every day," and, "Each person must exercise a particular amount of time per day." How many of you would say that it's absolutely asinine and ludicrous that I could go to jail for not eating the right amount of food or too much food? That would be a legislation of morality. However, when it came to this issue of homosexuality, we said, "Well, the church designed marriage. We came up with the name 'marriage,' and God came up with this whole idea, so we're going to force people to do what we want them to do." We have lost the battle of love over this issue of homosexuality. Andrew Marin said, "The political world means too much to Christianity and people mean too little,"[47] and I agree with him. The Lord at times handed the greater culture over to their desires (Rom. 1:24 and Ps. 81) because they proved they didn't want Him. Paul, in 1 Corinthians 5:12, even discusses this idea of "judging outsiders" when he states, "For what have I to do with judging outsiders? Is it not those inside the church whom you are to judge?" My point is that God is the judge, not us. People should matter to us more than our political persuasion. People should matter to us more than our stuff. Yet, sadly people are not as important in our economy as they are in God's economy.

The church should still be able to decide for itself, however, and not be told what to do by politicians. The church should still maintain her freedom, but not try to invoke her values through the political realm. I feel with the current battle about this idea of marriage, churches should be able to hold to their convictions that marriage is between a man and a woman. They should be able to choose. They shouldn't be forced to go against their beliefs in their particular church. Jesus is good because He loved us all enough not to force Himself upon us. He is good because He drew us to Himself, despite of our sin and mess. Jesus is good because He loves the LGBTQ community.

We've looked deeply into the response to this issue of homosexuality so far largely from the perspective of those not struggling with it personally. As we continue to look at this issue I want to look from both points of view—those not struggling with same-sex attraction and those who are struggling. When it comes to engaging this issue from those struggling, I see four responses that are possible.

GOING FOR A GIRL, WHEN I WANT A GUY

The first response is to seek heterosexual relations despite their homosexual inclinations. I know a guy who struggles with being gay,

---

47   Andrew Marin, *Love is an Orientation: Elevating the Conversation with the Gay Community*, (Downers Grove: IVP Books), 89.

but he felt the Lord's conviction upon him, and he was able to fall (emotionally) in love with a woman. Now, falling in love and being sexually attracted are different for him, and his wife understood how he felt. His wife understood that her husband was not experiencing a deep sexual attraction to her, but a deep emotional one. There is emotional pain for the wife that goes with her understanding, but they continue to walk through it. They have had kids together, and those kids are beautiful. He and his wife are still married and happily so; they found a way to live with his inclination for homosexuality, but yet remain happily married. However, here's the thing: that's not for everybody. Forcing someone to be in a heterosexual relationship despite his or her inclinations is ridiculous. If you say, "That's the only response you can have," that's wrong.

LIVING A CELIBATE LIFE

The next response a person struggling with same-sex attraction can have is celibacy. Some really wrestle with this particular response. But I believe that in 1 Corinthians 7:8, we see that a call to celibacy isn't a death sentence but a call to something noble. There are people who are heterosexual that are called to celibacy; this is not simply a call for those struggling with homosexuality. I have friends who are heterosexual who have been called to celibacy. These friends of mine acknowledge they are attracted to the opposite sex, but they feel God wants them to live in celibacy to do more work for Him they couldn't do married and with a family.

If you look at the Apostle Paul, he lived a celibate life. Yet he consistently talks about this issue of a thorn in his side. Many commentators believe that Paul is talking about a sexual attraction to women, that it was hard for him and he was struggling consistently. When he went into these different towns, there was a lot of prostitution and a lot of sexual messiness that was going on. If you're a guy who is attracted to women, and you walk into a town where there are naked women offering themselves to you for very low prices, that would be difficult—especially being single. Paul consistently asked God to take that thorn away. But God never took it away from him. I believe that God still called Paul to be celibate. At the end of 2 Corinthians 12, Paul says he realizes that his struggle was something he could understand God better in—his weakness. God comes forward stronger in our weaknesses. Paul used to be an arrogant Pharisee. If he didn't have a thorn in his side, he would have been a total tool. He would have been like, "I've got this Jesus thing down. I'm good to go." But God put this thing in Paul's life to cripple him a little bit to realize that he didn't have it together, but God did. So there are things in your life and my life that we're going to call thorns in our sides.

Celibacy is not the solution that you automatically offer first and say, "You have to do this." It's one of those things you say this is an option. This is not a situation where you kick them and tell them what they have to do. There needs to be a clear calling to this and a passionate desire to do as God asks.

I WILL LIVE GAY, AND GOD SAYS IT'S OKAY

The third option is to continue to seek homosexual relations and back it theologically. There is a huge group of people in the gay community that back their gay sexual conduct theologically, saying, "Theologically this is okay. Those certain portions of Scripture that many say says gay conduct is wrong. Well, we don't believe that is what God is saying. We don't think believing homosexuality is wrong is the right interpretation." Many of these people would say that the words translated really mean to have sex with little boys and not sex with men. "Pedophilia was what Paul was really talking about," they may say to justify this position. And there are all these different interpretations for what "certain words mean or don't mean." Now when someone has that interpretation, and they back it theologically, should it be our goal to try and battle them, duke it out, convict, or judge them for what they believe? Is that our role? No, but too often this is the game we play. We may sometimes walk around with this big haughty thing on our shoulders, but the reality is this: we are not the Holy Spirit.

For me, my personal conviction is that the Scripture means what it says. When it comes to homosexuality, the Scripture is clear. For thousands of years, commentators and scholars have interpreted the passages on homosexual conduct as sinful. Only in the last 150 years has there been this new interpretation towards a different meaning. That's why I say I can't get on board with this new interpretation. Even despite my disagreement with this new interpretation, I'm not going to consistently say people who believe homosexuality is okay are wrong, that I hate them, and that they shouldn't even come to my church. That response, however, is often how we treat homosexuality: reacting to people who believe differently from ourselves and having conversations with others. That's not what we are supposed to do. Later I'm going to share with you how disciples of Christ should react to false interpretations on this subject should be.

I WILL LIVE GAY AND FORGET GOD

The fourth response of those who struggle with the gay lifestyle is that they reject God entirely. This is the saddest reality we have in our entire history with this issue. Because of the way the church and Christians as a whole have responded to homosexuality, many people have left their entire Christian life for the gay community where they find the love and identity that they have never found in the Christian church. My friends, that needs to change, and it's you who can change that. Your generation gets this issue better than many have before. You get the understanding of loving and walking alongside, even in the mess of life. Many in our generation have seen the hypocrisy in the church. When people's lives are a wreck and they need the Body of Christ the most, the Body rejects them. I have seen this personally as well. I was a pastor's kid. My mother divorced my dad, married some drunkard, and everyone in our church walked away from her as if she was a pariah. She had the scarlet letter upon her chest and was no good to anyone. When I was a pastor, I said that would not happen in the church I was a part of because that's not how we should respond through the gospel.

As we look at this from both the perspective of those wrestling with gay inclinations as well as those who do not, how should those not wrestling with it respond to those who are? We've looked at how those who do not struggle are to see the issue, but how do we respond to the people? This may very well be one of the most important points to catch in this whole topic of homosexuality.

YOU'RE GAY? I'M DONE WITH YOU

I believe that Christians who are not struggling with same-sex attraction have three different reactions to homosexuality. Walking away is the first response we could have. We could say, "Okay, you are a mess; you're terrible, awful, and have this struggle. I cannot be around you until you are fixed." For the last seventy years that has been the church's response many times—that you need to get this right before you come to God. Well how am I going to get it right if I am not with God? You tell someone, "Hey, I want you to go away and stop being a drunk and come back to church when you're all cleaned up. Do this on your own, with no support. We aren't going to help you." It seems ridiculous. But that's exactly what we do. We're not willing to walk in the mess. It's too strange and odd to us. This issue makes people uncomfortable and so instead of walking in the mess with people (as Jesus did), we walk away.

I'M TOLERANT

The other response is acceptance or tolerance. This word gets a bad rep. The word "tolerance" has been thrown around in so many different ways that I hate using the word, but I'm trying to use it so you see where I'm coming from. When we are asked the question "Is it a sin to be gay?" we need to make sure we are gentle in the way we delineate out "homosexual act" and the actual inclination to be attracted to the same sex. If we are not gentle with this delineation, here's what's going to happen: if we respond with a "Yes," many may automatically jump to a conclusion and say, "Ah that's my whole identity. You don't love me, and God doesn't love me. Everything I am is detestable to you and to God." So we have to make sure we are having a conversation that is real and honest. We *should* say, "Here's where I believe the sin is. Do I believe God doesn't love you because you do this thing? That's not what I believe, because I know that I'm a mess. I know that I'm on many of the lists in Scripture that describe detestable sins. Yet, I also know that God washed me. That's no longer my identity. It's what I wrestle with."

But if we say, "Oh, yeah, yeah. It's fine. Go ahead and do whatever you want to do," and we have a conviction in our heart that the act is sinful, then we're not doing them any favors. This is the response of tolerance: responding with an acceptance of their choice to be active in the act of homosexual sex, even though we may disagree. Culture teaches us this through the ideals of relativism and declares there are no absolutes. Culture says, "One person thinks it's okay, so don't judge their personal opinion on the matter."

LOVE AND GRACE FILLED WITH TRUTH

Finally, we can respond with love, filled with grace and truth. Even if they disagree with your interpretation of Scripture, rejection is never what we are called to do. We are called to walk in the mess of discovery with and alongside of them. Walking alongside is not consistently reminding them of their sin. When someone is telling you they are wrestling with a particular sin and come to church every Sunday, do you look at them every Sunday and ask, "Are you still sinning?"

Even if the person struggling or blatantly living in the homosexual lifestyle looks at you in the face and says they believe they are Christians, but they don't believe it's a sin, we *still* walk alongside them because we are not the judge and not the one who convicts—the Holy Spirit is. If you really believe that person is in sin, you don't sit there and consistently berate them about it; you pray for them and walk alongside them. You prepare yourself so if they have a question or are wrestling with temptation, you're not sitting there taking the hammer of God's Word and pounding them in the head. In this walking alongside approach, you are lovingly saying let's talk about this and have a conversation. I feel that this is a much better alternative to shoving them away or walking away from them.

Here is another thing that Christians do. Too often, many Christians talk without asking the Holy Spirit to speak through them. Too often when we start trying to bring people to Jesus, it's us bringing them to Jesus rather than Jesus bringing them to Himself. When talking about this topic of homosexuality as well, we don't consult the Spirit to speak to us and through us, we simply choose to go in guns blazing with whatever interpretation we feel is best. We don't ask Him to fill us with grace and truth, we go into these conversations on our own and end up wounding each other deeply.

On a larger scale as well, Christians have told the gay community that only their sexual behavior is worth discussing. Many times we label LGBTQ people as nothing more than a dysfunctional set of sexual attractions and behaviors rather than whole persons with unique stories to tell. I know a lot of my gay friends would say this is how they feel about the church and Christians in general—the only thing that matters is their sexual attraction. Their stories don't matter, nor who they are as people. The only thing that matters is their sexual preferences. That's all people want to talk about with them. So why would those who are wrestling with homosexuality or living in that lifestyle want to keep going to a place that consistently reminds them of the reason they are hated; so they don't go to that place—they don't go to church.

How do we respond well? One way is to remember that God is love and love is not a jerk (1 John 8:16). There are ways you and I respond to people that's jerky. We come off as jerks. Or in other non-Christian places, maybe we might say other words. Right? I don't want to get in trouble. God is love and love is not a jerk. We should respond with love. God didn't promise an end to temptation; He promised a way of escape. This is for all of us. In 1 Corinthians 10:15, God didn't say, "Hey, you're tempted with certain things and the temptation will go away." There is a way of escaping temptation however. We respond with that.

Our goal should be to direct gay people to Jesus and not to heterosexuality. Too often when this conversation comes up, our goal is to pray the gay away. There are actually Christian gay camps where parents will send their Christian kids and say they have to go to the ex-gay camp. And that tells that student or that child, that whatever you are, you're like an alien and you've got to go cast the alien out of you and be normal again. It's ridiculous. This is what we do. And we say, man, we've got to pray the gay away and start anointing people like we have or see people get straight. Our goal no matter what sin struggle we find people in is to direct people towards Jesus. And Jesus will be the one. If they have a chance to change their conviction of what the Bible says, it's Jesus' job to do that and not yours. Your job is to walk alongside, to love and encourage. And when they ask you about your biblical convictions, be honest. But even if they disagree with you, even if you have someone you desperately love and desperately walk with and you know they know Jesus and you know the gospel is all over them and they still have this thing that they don't think is wrong for them, we're still called to walk alongside them and to encourage them. We're still called to be there. Not to judge them and try to get them to be what we want them to.

We're to lead them towards Jesus. How often do you and I do that? With our friends that struggle with any sin. When someone is struggling with a sin, how often do we want to pray that sin away? And how often are we leading them to the Cross of Jesus and saying only by the power of the Holy Spirit can you really get with this. If you're really convicted and really want to change, I can't force you to, you can't force you to, only God can help you to. We're not called to be the judge or enforce God's rules, we are called to love.

Reverend Billy Graham answered a question about why he still supported president Bill Clinton after his sexual stuff. And he said this: "It is the Holy Spirit's job to convict, God's job to judge, and my job to love." Are we to encourage, admonish, and speak truth? Yes, we are, but while filled with grace, gentleness, and respect. 1 Peter 3:15 says, "But in your hearts honor Christ the Lord as holy, always being prepared to make a defense to anyone who asks you for a reason for the hope that is in you; yet do it with gentleness and respect." Here's a really big challenge to all of us in the room. No matter what you are struggling with in your lifestyle, if you are not honoring Christ as Lord in your life, you should not be talking to other people about theirs. That's huge. The first part of that is "In your hearts, honor Christ the Lord as holy." Are you honoring Christ in your heart?

Finally, remember this: no matter how much we might want something for a LGBTQ person, their convictions and beliefs are always up to them. And we have to be okay in the tension. We want it resolved now! God the Father is the judge and God the Holy Spirit is the one who convicts. Those jobs do not belong to us, so we need to stop trying to do them.

You may be reading this as one who is secretly struggling with this issue and have been afraid to talk to anyone about it. I'll talk to you. Follow me on Twitter @marv_nelson and send me a message. Don't remain hidden and feeling alone. No matter what you decide in the end, I won't reject you.

As we close this chapter, there are two books I want to encourage you to read. The first is *Love is an Orientation: Elevating the Conversation with the Gay Community.* This book was written by a heterosexual male who has spent the last thirteen years of his life living in an LGBTQ community—purposefully loving and walking alongside them, not trying to judge, push, or force anything upon anyone, but rather saying there is a different church response and a different response that Jesus gives to the gay community. This is a book you should read to understand how to respond to the gay community because many doing a really bad job. I'm saying the church has done a very bad job.

The next one is *Washed and Waiting*. The conversation about celibacy is all through this book. Wesley Hill is a Christian and a seminary professor who teaches at a seminary near me in Pittsburgh. His book is a conversation about his journey of celibacy in the midst of his being gay. Now it might not be a book for everyone to read right away if you are wrestling with gay inclinations or wrestling with a gay lifestyle. But that's what it's about.

These are great books to start off with. They both point to the reality that Jesus is good in the midst of this situation.

Jesus loves the gay community and this is a very important conversation to continue to have and learn about. We must see though that Jesus *is* good, and even if His followers have done a poor job at being good and loving, He has not!

REFLECTIONS ON "JESUS LOVES THE LGBTQ COMMUNITY"

1. What are your thoughts on the four responses of those struggling with homosexuality mentioned?

2. What are your thoughts on the three responses of those not struggling mentioned?

3. What do you wrestle with the most as it pertains to this issue?

4. How can you allow Christ's design for love and sex to change the way in which you see this issue?

JESUS LEFT HIS BODY BEHIND

WHEN ONE ASKS ANOTHER: "WHAT are your thoughts on church?" the response in today's culture is generally a mixed bag of thoughts, most likely filled with negative vibes. Where the church was once the epicenter of society, it, today, ranks very low on the list of "happy thoughts" for your average American or European. The church in many respects has lost the ability to speak into current culture and instead has faced inwardly upon themselves: missing the point of being sent out.

Despite the current "church norm," Christ has set up the church to be the hope of the nations. The church is the very Body of Christ to this world, and the church is to incarnate (be the flesh of) Christ to this world. Jesus is good because He has left us His Body! Maybe you're asking, "Why would this, or how could this, ever be good when the church in many ways has done some harm to this world?"

The church, both the local and the universal, are called to be the Body of Christ, of which He is the head (Eph. 1:22-23 and 1 Cor. 12:27). This would suggest that the mission and purpose of the church would be the same as that of Christ Jesus. The church is called to walk the earth as Jesus did, to teach the way Christ did, and seek that which Christ sought. Christ's time on earth was full of mission and purpose; He made it clear what His mission and purpose were! He was not one to sugarcoat His reasoning or hide His true purpose; He put it all out on the line.

Here is a list of things He said of Himself and why He came: He "came to seek and save that which is lost" (Luke 19:10); "came to serve, rather than be served" (Mark 10:45 and Phil. 2); "be the doctor for the sick" (Matt. 9:12); came to make disciples (Matt. 28:18); and "humble himself to death on a cross" (Phil. 2).

These are only *some* of the purpose and mission that Christ came to fulfill. When He was leaving this earth, Jesus gave the church a specific mission: "And Jesus came and said to them, 'All authority in heaven and on earth has been given to me. Go therefore and make disciples of all nations, baptizing them in the name of the Father and of the Son and of the Holy Spirit, teaching them to observe all that I have commanded you. And behold, I am with you always, to the end of the age" (Matt. 28:18-20).

What does this reduce the church's mission and purpose down to? I believe that through the Scriptures we can boil down our mission and purpose to this list, which we should accomplish through the power of the Holy Spirit: be a unified Body of believers under one head, Christ, who seeks out and saves the lost (Matt. 9:12; Luke 19:10); develop new believers into disciples who make disciples (evangelize, baptize, and teach) (Matt. 28:18-19); heal the sick and broken (James 5); aid the poor, feed the hungry (James 2); take care of widows and orphans (James 1); desire to serve rather than to be served (Mark 10:45 and Phil. 2); and love God with all your heart, soul, and mind and love your neighbor as yourself (Luke 10:27). The church is to be a sent people (more on this later), not a people who cluster up into "Holy Huddles" just sitting and awaiting Christ's return. The church is to be a people who pour themselves out like a drink offering to the world, not a selfish band of consumers.

These are all admonitions from Scripture and Christ Himself. They are *not* at all easy to carry out, which is why Christ sent us the promised Holy Spirit! In and of ourselves, we would absolutely fail at this job. We are imperfect people trying to lead imperfect people to Holiness. For this very reason, Christ sent the Holy Spirit into our midst, so we could, as He did, live by the Spirit. It is my firm belief that Christ came as fully man and fully God, but did His miracles using the Holy Spirit. We, as His Body, could use Him as an example as to how we can tap into the power that the Holy Spirit has for our lives, but sadly, I don't believe we tap into the power we have.

As stated before, Christ is the head of the church, as a husband is the head of his household. Ephesians 5:23b says: *"Christ is the head of the church, his body, and is himself its Savior"* (emphasis mine). So then, what is the church's relationship to Christ with Him as the head? This means that the church is constantly looking to Christ to guide them, lead them, and transform them. Two great things mentioned already can assist in this: following the example of Christ while He was on earth and listening to the Spirit of God. The church is the Bride of Christ! He has wooed us, called us, and wed us as His own. Revelation 9 speaks of the wedding of Christ to His bride and that bride is the church. We are to be in constant relationship with Him, hearing His voice, following His leading, and going to the ends of the earth to proclaim Him among the nations.

There's a story I just read about a man who finds himself in the valley of the blind. He can see, but these kind and gentle people don't even know what *see* means—for twelve generations they've been blind. When he comes into the valley talking about sight, vision, eyes, and *seeing*, the blind people mock him, despise him, and say he's an idiot. "There are no such words. There is no such thing," they say.

Yet he can see and they are blind. A doctor comes to examine this *seeing* man and comes to realize that the protruding things he calls eyes are the cause for this man's insanity and in order to cure him the eyes must be cut off. These people didn't have eyes, they had sunken sockets, so they knew nothing of protruding eyes like the young man did. He was an odd ball to them, weird, insane, and made no sense because they were blind. *He was their hope to understanding the beauty of things seen, but many of them refused to even give him the opportunity to speak.*

You see, as Christians, we are the seeing man among the blind community. To many, our seeing, eyes and sight, sounds weird, dumb, and idiotic. Many people can't interact with the message because to those blind for generations—the words don't even exist in their vocabulary.

In order to speak to the blind community, this young man needed to engage them on their level of understanding and slowly bring them to the understanding of sight and what it means to see.

We have the same task before us, to incarnate ourselves within the community of the blind in order to get them to see. How do we do this? How does this connect to the *missio dei* or the mission of God? I believe the answer is it is the *missio dei!*

Many have dubbed it "missional" because it is the very mission God has given us and showed us how to do it best.

So, we are forced to ask these questions: What is Missional? And Why Missional? Alan Hirsch, one of the biggest voices in today's church culture, said, "Missional church is a community of God's people that defines itself by, and organizes its life around, its real purpose of being an agent of God's mission to the world."[48] Reading through John 1:1-5 and 14-18 and seeing the mission of God displayed in the incarnation, I think we can grab some great keys to why we should be missional.

I. THE WORLD IS BLIND (JOHN 1:5, 18)

The beautiful story of the mysterious incarnation is remarkable to think about, audacious to believe, but 100% true. God became man and dwelt among us, and He did this to shine light into the darkness. Due to original sin, we humans were now born blind as the community of the blind was. Sight was no longer even known to us a few generations down the line, yet God in His mercy and love desired for us to see once again.

The problem with a lot of evangelism today is that many well-meaning Christians know they can see and those they are sharing with are blind, but *Christians do not use the experience of incarnation to show the blind their blindness.* Instead, today's Christians try to reason

---

48   Alan Hirsch, *Right Here, Right Now: Everyday Mission for Everyday People* (Grand Rapids: Baker Books, 2011), 66.

with the blind, trying to show them their blindness by mere words and arguments. If the unsaved are blind, just as the blind community in our story and have had generations of blindness, they will think our words idiotic and will dismiss them as the blind men did the young man who could see. *We can't argue a blind man into sight!* We must lead them to the great God who can do the miraculous work of healing and opening the eyes. We are seed planters; God does the miraculous work!

We are light to their darkness. This can only be done best life-on-life. We must place ourselves among the blind communities, live there, rest there, and commune there among the blind. Enter their space (not their blindness). Know them, know their ways, love them, and gently display light before them.

What drives me bonkers is that this way of thinking is why we send out missionaries to Africa or Saudi Arabia or China, this very idea of incarnation, is what drives us to missions. Yet here, in our backyard, we try to have holy separatist huddles and blitz the blind with "sight" campaigns. We look crazy, foolish, and idiotic all the while enforcing to them that their way of living is better.

II. GOD IS OUR EXAMPLE (JOHN 1:14-16)

Jesus was the first missionary, sent on mission from God to be God in the flesh—to dwell among us and to be with us and lovingly direct us to Himself—where we would find healing, restoration, redemption, forgiveness, and life. He then sent His Spirit to indwell us so we can continue His mission of dwelling among the world and continue His mission to lovingly direct us to Himself, the only place we would find healing, restoration, redemption, forgiveness and life! He was the example of how to do it, why to do it, and what it looks like to do it. If God did it, I think we should be doing the same, don't you?

III. CHRISTIAN MEANS: INCARNATION OF CHRIST (ACTS 11:23-26)

This reality for us as a church is so vital to understand because it resets our expectations of ourselves, of our lives, and of our missions, letting us see the macro vision of God, rather than continuing in the micro vision. Christian is more than a "religious" title. The name is a formation of identity because we are saying when we claim to be "Christian," that we are a small replication of Jesus Himself. We are the incarnation of God to this dark world. We are the eyes to the blind. We purposely choose to take this on and it changes our lives in every way. It can't just be something that's practiced on Sunday and once in a while everywhere else. It can't be a minor reality; it is the whole reality. Will we fail? YES, but God gives grace in those moments. Yet, His mission redirects our very way of living because we are in fact the incarnation of Christ. We are always on a mission field attempting to love the broken people around us and picking a particular group to focus on being the incarnation of Christ to them! It could be engineering students or it could be the nursing students. In the future it could be the nurses, doctors, teachers, tradesmen, or whomever you work with and for. Once we see ourselves as constant missionaries, we choose our words, actions, and attitudes differently.

Here's something that might make people mad, but I think it's worth exploring, even if you think I'm wrong. In order to be the best missionaries we can, we must choose our people group and incarnate Jesus among them rather than the random evangelism blitzes that have been done and are continuing to be done. Jesus incarnated Himself as a Jew, to Jews among Jews. He talked with Gentiles, and spent some time with them, but His main focus was the Jews. Paul then felt the need to incarnate Jesus among the Gentiles. Missionaries from our denomination choose Africans, Chinese, or whatever people group they desire to incarnate Jesus to. Why do we do it differently? Why do we try and bring the gospel to people we don't know and can't relate to and ignore the ones we are closest to?

"The church exists to equip and mobilize Christ followers to embody Christ's mission. . . . Mission is the difference between having an emotion and actually doing something about it."[49]

---

49   Steve Saccone and Cheri Saccone, *Protégé: Developing Your Next Generation of Church Leaders* (Downers Grove: InterVarsity Books, 2012) 22.

The reality is that we don't have a choice but to be on mission if we are to adhere and hold to the teachings of Jesus. He calls us to be incarnational, and He sends us.

IV. THE CHURCH IS A SENT PEOPLE (JOHN 20:21; MATTHEW 28:18-19)

David Bosch, a great missionary, once said, "The classical doctrine on the *missio dei* as God the Father sending the Son, and God the Father and the Son sending the Spirit was expanded to include yet another 'movement': Father, Son and Holy Spirit sending the church into the world." We are sent into the world to incarnate Jesus. We should all have a different focus group tailored to how God has wired us. For me, it's college students. Who has God been laying on your heart? What is your major in school? What job do you hope to have? That is most likely who God is sending you to and right now. Who do you spend time with that needs the incarnation of Jesus? Have you been living in accordance to God's mission?

We are a sent people. We are to be among those we are sent to *and gently, lovingly share with them the amazing awesomeness of sight*. **We must be their Jesus experience, leading them to Him all the while.** Describing Him, living as He would, talking as He would, loving as He would, and showing them the healing for their blindness as He did for us!

I know I went in and out of "we" and "they" language, but being a follower of Christ and a member of the Body that He left, I must identify with the church and claim a "we" stance because the message is for myself as well. The question still lingers as to what good is Jesus? The answer is that He didn't leave the world and wash His hands of it. He purposefully left His church (His Body) so that the mission of saving the lost and bringing sight to the blind could continue.

Many people who claim faith in Christianity will then ask the "how" question, and I think 1 Peter 3:15 gives some practical answers to this question. That passage says: "But in your hearts honor Christ the Lord as holy, always being prepared to make a defense to anyone who asks you for a reason for the hope that is in you; yet do it with gentleness and respect."

We must make Christ Lord in our hearts, not just our Savior, but also our Lord.

Second, we must be gentle and respectful to others and their beliefs. If we expect them to listen to us, we must listen to them as well.

Third, we must *never* enter in to argument mode. We can't fight for Jesus—trust me; He can handle it Himself. We are to live and talk Jesus to people. We can share our faith when they ask questions about why our lives are different, because they will ask if we made Christ our Lord!

If we choose one person (not as a project) whom we will share Jesus with, it can change the world!

If we were to begin today with a "gospel tent meeting" approach, bringing in 1,000 non-Christians and presenting the Gospel to them— once in the morning, once in the afternoon, and once in the evening (3,000 per day), it would take 5,014 years to reach the *present* world's population (not counting all those who will be born in the next 5014 years). If we chose to seek out one person a year and challenge them to do the same, the exponential growth would be much quicker than that of the tent meeting approach.

The main reason why the question "What good is Jesus?" is even being asked is because His body has been failing at being His Body. The church as a whole has not embodied the mission and purpose Christ sent us out to embody. In many respects, we've wounded more than we've healed, and we must stop the wounding and re-embrace Christ's call on our life as the church. If you've been wounded by the church in the past and have been asking the question: "What good is Jesus?" in your life due to those wounds, I am sorry. As a pastor in the church, I apologize to you right now on the text of this page and boldly state that your wounds are most likely not from a good expression of Christ, and I know you deserved better than that. I pray right now that the Lord Himself, the Lord of all Comfort, will heal your heart now as you read this so you can know He is good. Christ is good because He left us His body. May we begin to be the full expression of Jesus *now* to this world, so they can experience the real Jesus who is very good!

REFLECTIONS ON "JESUS LEFT
HIS BODY BEHIND"

1. Why do YOU think the church exists?

2. How well has the church been about "why it exists" according to this chapter?

3. Why do you think the church has struggled to stay on mission?

4. How can you help the church stay on mission?

AFTERWORD

IN ITS DYSFUNCTION, THIS WORLD cannot bring all that we need. Christ alone brings satisfaction. All of us in this world long to be satisfied. There is a deep searching for satisfaction. We desire to cling to those things that are good.

The key ingredient to finding the full goodness of Jesus is surrender. Everything in the Christian life flows from surrender as well. We must surrender to this idea that He is all we need. The Apostle Paul lived this way. The Apostle Peter lived this way, as did many others who have gone before us. David Benner states, "The core of surrender is voluntarily giving up our will. Only love can induce us to do this. But even more remarkable, not only can love make it possible, it can make it almost easy."[50] What's interesting is that our heart actually desires surrender. Our deepest longing in satisfaction is being able to give our whole self to someone or something. We long to not be alone, we desire to fully trust and lean into another. However, we must learn this fact: *Love is the impetus for surrender.* Once we are hit with the fullness of God's love, surrender becomes easy, as Benner states. Benner then goes on to say, "Only God deserves absolute surrender, because only God can offer absolutely dependable love."[51] Paul found this to be true of Christ and encouraged the churches in his care and us to seek to find our satisfaction in only Christ and we can do this fully by surrendering everything into His hands. The Father brings perfect satisfaction to our souls because He brings perfect love. Only He can offer this gift, thus only He can satisfy.

---

50   David Benner, *Surrender to Love: Discovering the Heart of Christian Spirituality* (Downers Grove: InterVarsity Books, 2003) 59.

51   Ibid.

This gift, however, is not a one and done process, but a continual one. We will get distracted and our hearts will wander from the heart of God. We will then once again fall into the trap of seeking temporal things to fulfill and eternal longing. Satisfaction is continuously seeking to *know* God.

Jesus is good because He gives us the ability through His death and resurrection to truly *know* God. His death was the ultimate act of love on our behalf. My hope is that you've been able to see the answers to the seemingly simple question "What good is Jesus?" and experience maybe even a small portion of His deep love for you through it. If you have experienced His love in the midst of this, I encourage you to surrender to His love and allow His Spirit to lead, guide, and direct your path. Then you will not only have cognitive answers to the goodness of Jesus, but tangibly experience His goodness in the totality of your life.

For more information about
Marvin Nelson
&

What Good Is Jesus?
please visit:
www.marvnelson.com
pstrmarv@icloud.com
@marv_nelson
www.facebook.com/PastorMarv

For more information about
AMBASSADOR INTERNATIONAL
please visit:

www.ambassador-international.com
@AmbassadorIntl
www.facebook.com/AmbassadorIntl